W9-AQZ-235

(62 - 15376)

3-19-63
11-11-63

AMERICAN AUTHORS
AND CRITICS SERIES

GENERAL EDITORS

JOHN MAHONEY, University of Detroit
FOSTER PROVOST, Duquesne University

ABOUT THE AUTHOR

GEORGE HOCHFIELD is Assistant Professor of English at
The Ohio State University, and was a Fulbright Lecturer
in American Literature at the Universities of Bologna and
Venice, 1958. Professor Hochfield edited *The Great Secession Winter and Other Essays* by Henry Adams.

Bettmann Archive

Henry Adams

B
A

HENRY ADAMS

An Introduction and Interpretation

GEORGE HOCHFIELD
Ohio State University

Barnes & Noble, Inc.   New York
Publishers   Booksellers   Since 1873

WINGATE COLLEGE LIBRARY
WINGATE, N. C.

©
Copyright, 1962
By Barnes & Noble, Inc.
All rights reserved

L. C. Catalogue Card Number: 62–15370

PRINTED IN THE UNITED STATES OF AMERICA

PREFACE

EVERY STUDENT of Henry Adams comes sooner or later to feel that the *Education,* the book with which Adams makes his strongest claim to prominence in American literary history, is the greatest obstacle to a proper understanding of the man and his work. The *Education,* in some respects, is a fascinating deception; it seems to offer unreserved self-disclosure, but it is so stylized and so qualified by irony that it ends by creating a myth. The myth is indispensable in its own way, for it is a product of Adams' imagination, but it is not the whole, or even the essential, truth about Henry Adams.

In order to correct the impression left by the *Education,* it is necessary to place that book in a perspective which includes the rest of Adams' literary career. He was a prolific and exceptionally varied writer, and everything he did is touched with his genius. And, as with all writers, there is a continuity and development of thought in his intellectual history which relate his books to one another in a coherent order. The primary object of this study is to demonstrate the continuity of Adams' mind in his books, and to define the order of relation among them. My method of procedure is to analyze each work separately, to uncover what seem to me its fundamental motives and central meanings, and to establish its connections with the unifying themes of Adams' whole career. My own assumption is that the best way to understand Adams is by treating him as an artist, by reading his work with the deliberate attention to formal structure, connotation, and nuance that all serious literary art deserves.

I wish to express my gratitude to the following publishers: Sagamore Press, Inc. for permission to reprint parts of my introduction to *The Great Secession Winter and Other Essays* by Henry Adams; Houghton Mifflin Company for permission to quote from *The Education of Henry Adams* and *Mont-Saint-Michel and Chartres* by Henry Adams, *A Cycle of Adams Letters 1861–1865* and *Letters of Henry Adams 1858–1918,* both edited by Worthington C. Ford, and *Henry Adams and His Friends,* edited by Harold Dean Cater; and The Macmillan Company for permission to quote from *The Degradation of the Democratic Dogma* by Henry Adams, edited by Brooks Adams; Constable & Company Ltd. for permission to quote from *The Life of George Cabot Lodge* and *The Education of Henry Adams.* I am indebted to Professor James D. Hart of the University of California under whose direction this book took its earliest form, and to former Ambassador John Davis Lodge and former Ambassador Henry Cabot Lodge for permission to quote from *The Life of George Cabot Lodge.*

G.H.

21263

CONTENTS

ILLUSTRATIONS

CHRONOLOGY

1838 Henry Brooks Adams born February 16, in Boston, Massachusetts, the fourth of five children of Charles Francis Adams and Abigail Brown Brooks. His maternal grandfather was Peter Chardon Brooks, the wealthiest Bostonian of his time. His paternal grandfather was John Quincy Adams, sixth President of the United States, whose father was John Adams, second President of the United States.

1848 Death of John Quincy Adams after his collapse on the floor of the House of Representatives.

1854–1858 Attended Harvard College where his earliest publications appeared in *The Harvard Magazine*. Delivered the Class Day Oration, June, 1858.

1858 Sailed for Europe in the fall to study Civil Law at the University of Berlin, a short-lived project. His father elected to Congress from the Third Massachusetts District.

1859–1860 Moved to Dresden. Traveled in Europe and sent letters to Boston papers, including an interview with Garibaldi from Palermo. Returned to the United States in October. Went to Washington with his father, who had been re-elected to Congress, in the capacity of private secretary, and sent correspondence to the Boston *Daily Advertiser* concerning political affairs during the secession winter.

1861–1868 Lived in London and served as private secretary to his father, who had been appointed Minister to Great Britain by President Lincoln. Wrote as anonymous correspondent to the New York *Times* until January, 1862, on diplomatic relations and British reactions to the Civil War. Began his first serious attempts at historical writing, which led to the publication of three articles in issues of the *North American Review* of 1867.

1868–1870 The "Washington experiment." Wrote as a free-lance political journalist for the *Nation* and the *North American Review*.

1870 Became assistant professor of medieval history at Harvard and editor of the *North American Review*.

1871 Published with his brother, Charles F. Adams, Jr., *Chapters of Erie and Other Essays*, containing previously printed articles.

1872 Married Marian Hooper, June 27, and began a year-long wedding trip that included Europe and a journey up the Nile.

1876 Edited *Essays in Anglo-Saxon Law*, which included the doctoral dissertations of three of his students (Henry Cabot Lodge among them) and an essay of his own, "Anglo-Saxon Courts of Law." Resigned the editorship of the *North American Review*.

1877   Edited *Documents Relating to New England Federalism, 1800–1815.* Gave up teaching and moved to Washington.

1879   Published *The Life of Albert Gallatin* and an edition of Gallatin's *Writings.* Began work on the *History of the United States during the Administrations of Jefferson and Madison.*

1880   Published *Democracy An American Novel* anonymously. It had a considerable *succès de scandale* and remained his most popular work during his lifetime.

1882   Published *John Randolph* in the American Statesmen Series, and wrote a life of Aaron Burr which never appeared but was probably incorporated in the *History.*

1884   Published *Esther* under the pseudonym Frances Snow Compton. The first quarter of the *History* was privately printed to safeguard the manuscript and facilitate its correction.

1885   Second quarter of the *History* printed. Suicide of Marian Adams, December 6, in their Washington home.

1886   Traveled to Japan with the painter John La Farge.

1888   Third quarter of the *History* put into print.

1889–1891   First two volumes of the trade edition of the *History* brought out in October, 1889. Four more volumes were issued the following year, and the last three, printed from manuscript, appeared in January, 1891.

1890–1892   Starting in August, 1890, traveled with La Farge to Hawaii, Samoa, Tahiti, Fiji, Australia, Ceylon, and Europe, returning to the United States in February, 1892.

1891   Published *Historical Essays,* mostly a reprinting of earlier pieces.

1893   Privately printed *Memoirs of Marau Taaroa, Last Queen of Tahiti,* which was later revised and reprinted in Paris, 1901, as *Memoirs of Arii Taimai E.* Elected, in absentia, President of the American Historical Association for 1894.

1894   Received the Loubat Prize for his *History* from Columbia University. Traveled in Cuba and Mexico. During the 1890's he became an inveterate wanderer and spent much of his time abroad, ranging from the Near East to Russia and Scandinavia. For many years he kept an apartment in Paris.

1902   *Mont-Saint-Michel and Chartres* completed in December. It was privately printed in 1904 and distributed to close friends as a New Year's gift. A trade edition was issued in 1913.

1906   Finished *The Education of Henry Adams,* of which a few copies were printed the following year and sent to friends and persons mentioned in the text for comment and correction.

1908   *The Rule of Phase Applied to History* written and offered to the *American Historical Review* early in 1909. It was refused for publication.

1910   *A Letter to American Teachers of History* printed and sent to professors of history at various universities. Almost none replied.

1911   Published *The Life of George Cabot Lodge* as a companion volume to the works of the poet.

1912   Suffered a heart attack in April and was seriously ill throughout the summer.

1914   Was in France at the outbreak of the World War, but managed to escape safely to England.

1918   Died in Washington, March 27, and was buried beside his wife in Rock Creek Cemetery. The *Education* was published under the auspices of the Massachusetts Historical Society and became a bestseller.

1919   *The Degradation of the Democratic Dogma,* titled and edited by Brooks Adams, was issued, containing "The Tendency of History," the *Rule,* and the *Letter.*

&s§ THE WASHINGTON EXPERIMENT

WHEN Henry Adams returned to the United States from England
in July, 1868, he was just such an "interesting case" as might
have been imagined by his friend of later years, Henry James. A young
man of thirty, a member of one of the most distinguished of American
families, having spent seven years in "the dreadful, delightful city" of
London as private secretary to his father, the American minister, comes
back to his native land in quest of a career. Needless to say, he is
talented and full of promise. His social connections extend from the
political and intellectual aristocracy of Boston to the United States
Congress, the Cabinet, and the Supreme Court. His consciousness is
perhaps as fine an instrument of response to life as may be found in
the Anglo-Saxon world, steeped in ancient New England habits of
moral earnestness and self-awareness, in the grand, unprovincial political tradition of the Adamses, and in the manners, the style, the currents of thought circulating in London, the world's most modern and
civilized metropolis. Above all, he is eminently "available," ready and
free for the first time in his life to subject himself "to the chances, the
complications of existence." What will become of him? What will he
make of his rich possibilities?

Four months after his homecoming Adams took the first step in his
new condition of freedom. It was perhaps the most predictable of his
life: he went into politics. Or rather, he went to Washington to begin
the "experiment" which was to constitute the first stage of his literary
career. As a political writer he thought he might capitalize on his
talents and even—though he never openly expressed the desire—find
some access to the tangible power of government itself. He was, as he
well knew, following in the footsteps of his ancestors, and his Washington experiment was not only a crucial personal undertaking but a test
of the continuity of American life.

What equipment did Adams bring with him to Washington? A
rough sketch of his mind, preliminary to the examination of his first
important writings, would have to take into account at least four basic
elements. First, the heritage of New England Puritanism, attenuated

into habit and filtered through the rationalistic Unitarianism which
still flourished in Boston during Adams' formative years. To this heritage Adams owed his instinctive apprehension of history as a moral
and teleological drama and his equally instinctive assumption that the
purpose of the individual life must be defined as the fulfillment of
moral duty, or the achievement of what one is tempted to call by its
original Puritan name of "sanctification." These are the underlying
causes of that "Puritan conscience" with which Henry Adams was as
powerfully afflicted as any of his ancestors, and which drove him finally
to judge himself a "failure."

Modifying this inheritance from Puritanism was the special bent
given it by the hundred years involvement in politics of the Adams
family. With the Adamses the Puritan conscience became, so to speak,
thoroughly politicized. Moral judgment permeated their social thought;
good and evil, vice and virtue were the terms of their statecraft. The
Adams ideal of government was an imitation of the divine order; the
statesman's function was to create systems of government in accordance with the foreordained "unalterable rules" by which nations are
eternally regulated. For the statesman rational moral obligation was
perfectly united with obedience to the will of a rational God. The old
Puritan "economy of redemption" was converted by the Adamses into
a secular political economy with the Puritan conscience as its engine.

However, ancestral politics compensated for excessive moralism by
an unfailing largeness of view with respect to American issues. The
Adamses were justifiably proud of being more than New England
politicians; their scope was national, and their object was the success
of the great social experiment which had been proclaimed and initiated
by the Declaration of Independence and the Constitution. Consequently they abhorred partisanship and were forever trying to rise
above it for the sake of revolutionary consistency as well as what they
took to be the national interest. None of them but John Adams managed to remain a member of one party all his life, and he had more
enemies within the ranks of the Federalists than outside them. Thus
the experience of a hundred years prepared the way for Henry Adams'
Washington experiment, which was both a reforming sortie against the
corruption bred by parties and an attempt to force a discussion of
national interests in the light of moral and constitutional principles.

A third significant element of Henry Adams' mind in 1868 was his
awareness of the growing influence of science in the intellectual life of
Europe. Through his friendship in London with Sir Charles Lyell,
Adams had become well acquainted with the Darwinian theory of
evolution, especially in its bearings upon geological studies. More importantly, Adams had been profoundly interested by the newly emer-
gent theories of "social science" first adumbrated by Comte and given
a powerful impetus by Darwinism: "a Comtist, within the limits of

evolution" was how he eventually came to label himself in the *Education*. Other writers gave a distinct and permanent shape to the suggestive influence of Comte and Darwin. Ernest Samuels has amply shown how Adams' reading of John Stuart Mill, Herbert Spencer, and Henry Buckle in the early sixties created an impression that was to deepen over the years until it crowded almost everything else from his mind.[1] All these writers were struck by the possibility of converting history into a science, by which they generally meant the synthesis of history and the physical sciences. They hoped that the laws of matter and energy might become keys to the sequence of historical events and thus to the prediction of the future course of society. Adams was swept up by this vision so far as to write his brother in 1863 that "everything in this universe has its regular waves and tides. . . . I believe every part of organic nature will be brought some day within this law." Furthermore, "the laws which govern animated beings will be ultimately found to be at bottom the same with those which rule inanimate nature." This formula later became Adams' *idée fixe*, but in the sixties it was still largely a formula, one that held out the vague promise of imminent and stupendous generalizations and induced him occasionally to adopt a scientific manner toward American political questions. Nevertheless, it is clear that the polarity of moralist and scientist was firmly established in his mind at the time of his return from England, and the resulting tension between them was to be seen in some of its effects almost immediately.

The fourth element of Adams' mind necessary to mention here was —to use a striking phrase he applied to Thomas Jefferson—its "intellectual sensuousness." Jefferson revealed this quality, Adams said, in the "subtle feeling for artistic form" betrayed by his writings. Adams himself betrayed exactly the same feeling even in his earliest and least "artistic" literary work. During the year before his homecoming he published three essays in the *North American Review*, "Captaine John Smith," "British Finance in 1816," and "The Bank of England Restriction," and in all of them the "sensuousness" of his mind struggled somewhat desperately to assert itself against the uncongeniality of his materials. The struggle was inevitable, for Adams' Puritanism forced him, in the latter two articles at any rate, to choose the dullest and most technical of subjects. They were proof of his seriousness as a political writer. Yet everywhere in them one finds a concern for style, for polished phrasing and graceful sequence, for a manner not that of the scholarly pedant but of the gentlemanly scholar. This attention to style was, however, but the superficial expression of Adams' intellectual sensuousness. Underlying it was a true artistic impulse toward an imaginative rendering of experience, an impulse not unlike

[1] *The Young Henry Adams* (Cambridge: Harvard University Press, 1948).

that of Henry James, whose unique achievement, Adams thought, was to teach "the world to read a volume for the pleasure of seeing the lights of his burning-glass turned on alternate sides of the same figure." The contradictory forces in Adams were thus not two but three. Together with the Puritan politician and the scientist was the artist; the crosscurrents set up among these varying tendencies generated the fascinating energy and variety of his literary career.

◆§ §◆

Henry Adams remained in Washington for nearly two years, and there are many signs that they were among the happiest of his life. He was "up to the ears in politics and public affairs"; his friends were the group of "active and intelligent young men" in Congress, the Treasury Department, or on the press, who were eager for reform and "charmed" by the prospect of a fight. Like them he found the violence of political controversy exhilarating; his letters of this period are filled with a joyous ferocity that is utterly without bitterness. When "The Legal-Tender Act" appeared, for example, he told a friend, "I have brought all the respectable old fools of the country down on me by a mighty impudent article in the April *North American.* . . . Well! it certainly was savage!" But savagery was not the sum of his ambition. A better measure is the hope he expressed after the first "Session" was printed. Frankly modeling this article on Lord Robert Cecil's "review of politics" in the *London Quarterly,* Adams foresaw a comparable influence for his own work. "If the future goes straight," he said, "I will make my annual 'Session' an institution and a power in the land."

Yet the pleasures and anticipations of Washington life—a life Henry Adams thought of as "Bohemian"—must have been accompanied by considerable dissatisfaction or he would have given the "experiment" a longer trial. As it was, he let himself be persuaded by his family and President Eliot to leave Washington in September, 1870, and accept a professorship in history at Harvard. Politics was not completely abandoned, since he also became editor of the *North American Review* which he intended to use as a forum for liberal opinion. But practically, Adams' removal to Cambridge marked the end of his first career as journalist and the beginning of his second as historian.

Despite its brevity and inconclusiveness, his stay in Washington was a decisive experience for Adams. In the *Education* he classed it among his many "failures," an attempt to do what he was not fitted for in a time that was not fitted for him. But the four chapters of the *Education* devoted to Washington show how deep an impression this period left in his mind. It did so because Washington was the first real test of certain political attitudes and assumptions derived from his family background. This test resulted in a disillusionment that shook him loose from the family tradition and opened the way, ultimately, to a questioning of all values that pretended to give a meaning, not only to politics, but to history as well.

⊷⧽ ⧼⊶

The role that Henry Adams undertook to perform in Washington was an unusual one for his time, and this partly explains his insecurity in it. He was neither reporter nor correspondent, but what should probably be called a "critic of government," one who attempts to penetrate beneath the surface of the news to fundamental issues of policy and organization. His criticism, as well as his reforming zeal, was motivated largely by two standards of judgment. They were standards which he never explicitly defined and perhaps never even consciously thought about, but which he inherited almost as part of his biological make-up from the philosophic systems of his forebears.

In the first place, he assumed, as John Quincy Adams had put it, that "The eternal and immutable laws of justice and morality are paramount to all human legislation." It therefore followed that government was obliged to act in keeping with these laws; that legislation must be framed on them and policy guided by them; in short, that government was a moral agent designed to aid man in the achievement of "virtue." Hence the justification of governmental conduct was necessarily couched in moral terms, as were the criteria for evaluating that conduct. To Charles Francis Adams, Henry's father, it had been axiomatic that "The first and greatest qualification of a statesman . . . is the mastery of the whole theory of morals which makes the foundation of all human society." The "great and everlasting question," he thought, "in political as well as private life," was the question of right and wrong.

It is this assumption, however vague and ill-defined, which determines the character of Henry Adams' early criticism. Over and over the most damning argument he can think of against protectionism, or the spoils system, or the use of greenbacks unbacked by gold as legal tender is that they have the effect of breeding evil, of degrading the moral life of the community.

> This attempt on the part of the legislature to exercise the executive power, [he wrote of the spoils system in the essay on "Civil Service Reform"] has produced in Congress and in the country an indifference to strict rules of wrong and right, a contempt for personal dignity, a cynical assumption of official dishonesty, and a patient assent to the supposed necessity of corruption.

Government loses its highest sanction, its very reason for being, when it permits and even propagates such forms of immorality. Above all, the duty of those who govern is to keep in mind their responsibility to "the principles upon which all government and all society must ultimately rest." To ignore this responsibility is to threaten with meaninglessness and disaster the whole enterprise of government itself. "The inevitable effect of opening a permanent and copious source of corruption . . . must be that the people are undone."

The second assumption on which Adams' criticism of government was based concerns the role in American politics of the Constitution. To the Adamses the Constitution had always been, in John Quincy's words, a "revered instrument." During the Civil War, as Henry Adams watched the course of events from his post in England, one of his greatest fears was that the Constitution might suffer irreparable changes. At one point he wrote to his brother that when the war was over their task would be to bring the country "back to its true course," to a "respect for law and order and the Constitution," lest "we lose all our landmarks and go ahead like France with a mere blind necessity to get on, without a reason or a principle."

The virtue of the Constitution was that it embodied more perfectly than any other comparable document or system of government the moral law that for the Adamses transcended human legislation. It provided, therefore, a solid foundation for the happiness and well-being of the American union, since, as John Adams thought, "the virtues [of the best republics] have been the effect of [a] well-ordered constitution, rather than the cause." From the time that John Adams proclaimed the Constitution the result of "the greatest single effort of national deliberation that the world has ever seen," he and his descendants were committed to protecting its integrity and founding on it their highest national ambitions.

This attitude toward the Constitution was responsible for many of Henry Adams' specific criticisms in his Washington essays. His denunciation of party machines, and his concern over the activities of great corporations like the Erie Railroad, came from his belief that their power was wholly extra-constitutional and hence a danger to the traditional structure of American government. Similarly, the decay of the executive power and the corruption of the legislature, which are alluded to in almost every one of the essays, are viewed by Adams with the dismay of one who sees something like an ideal form dissolving before his eyes. There is an unholy conspiracy which Adams is repeatedly dragging out into the light, a conspiracy among senatorial ambition, parties, and special interest "rings" which threatens to reduce constitutional government to a mere shadow and to erect in its place, "without a reason or a principle," a system of irrational power. Thus Adams' criticism, in large measure, was a conservative attempt to redefine the Constitution in terms of the problems of his own age, while its reforming purpose was to eradicate the immoral practices which had grown up like weeds in the cracks of the neglected Constitution.

❧ ❧

The disillusionment that began during his stay in Washington remained an active process in Henry Adams' mind for many years, and its consequences may be studied in such later works as *Democracy*, the *History of the United States of America during the Administrations of Thomas Jefferson and James Madison*, and the *Education*. But its earliest manifestations are visible in some of the essays he wrote while still in Washington. Most significant is the gradually hardening conviction, which is fully and explicitly stated in the second and last "Session," devoted to the legislative year 1869–70, that the moral purport of the Constitution was being lost, probably for good and all. The implications of this discovery for Adams, as may easily be imagined, were far-reaching. In the first place, it brought home to him that the Constitution had no special dispensation of Providence, that the ideal it had attempted to realize of a government powerless to encroach on the liberties of the people was "delusive" and "chimerical." "The great political problem of all ages cannot," he decided, "at least in a community like that of the future America, be solved by the theory of the American Constitution." But even more important, the failure of the Constitution threw into grave doubt the very basis of Adams' criticism. For if the moral order that the Constitution had tried to establish was impermanent and incapable of perfecting itself, what became then of the moral law transcending human legislation, the theory of which was supposed to be at the foundation of all human society? Evidently it was possible that society might not, after all, be grounded in moral law, and that the transcendent principles to which human legislators were ultimately responsible might themselves be delusive and chimerical. If this were so, what meaning was to be discerned in politics other than that contained in its superficial aspect, "the crash and war of jealous and hostile interests"? What ground existed outside the self on which the criticism and reform of politics might be firmly based?

Adams was forced to confront these disturbing questions by one notable deficiency in his critical point of view. When one searches his Washington essays for the ends implicit in them, the political objectives toward which they might be said to have been aiming, one must conclude that so far as Adams thought about the matter the only end he could conceive was simply the preservation of the Constitution in and for itself. Thus no alternatives were available to his mind once he became convinced that the Constitution was defunct. His ancestors, closer to the revolutionary vision of the early republic, had combined their faith in the Constitution with a faith in the social and intellectual progress of mankind under the beneficent influence of liberty, education, and the guarantee of inalienable rights. An ideal of man in full realization of his human possibilities, "a being of loftier port, of larger dimensions, of infinitely increased and multiplied powers, and of heavier and deeper responsibilities," animated the Republicanism of John Quincy Adams. But this clear outline was mostly lost to his grandson, for whom there remained only the moral compulsion inherent in such idealism without belief in the ideal itself; a sense of the necessity of commitment to principles without a clear idea of the object such principles were necessary for. Without a well-defined end, and forced, as he thought, to acknowledge the collapse of the Constitution, Adams saw his vague and unexamined assumption of a moral order transcending human law put to a test it could not possibly survive. The result was a loss, for the time being at any rate, of the critical motive, and a sense of life's meaninglessness in the absence of impersonal values that could legitimately claim the allegiance of faith and action. This state of mind is attested to by a variety of evidence: by Adams' relatively quick capitulation to the family pressure that favored his return from Washington to Boston; by remarks such as the following in his Washington letters, written at moments when he seemed to be quite happily embroiled in his journalistic adventures: "Personally I am still at a loss to know what the devil I want, or can possibly get, that would be an object, in case my friends came into power. . . . I want nothing and fight only for the amusement of fighting"; and by the feeling which emerged at this time and deepened over the years, particularly after the failure of the Independent Republican movement, that politics in the usual sense was sheer anarchy, a senseless struggle for power. In short, the outcome of Adams' "Washington experiment" was something in the nature of an intellectual crisis, not abrupt and violent, but subtle, protracted, and demanding of profound readjustments for its solution.

What that solution was, or whether it ever was achieved, are questions to be dealt with later in this book. But something may be said here concerning the effects of this crisis on Adams' mind, effects which more or less conditioned his quest for a solution. In the first place, he was impelled towards history as a possible means of clarifying the disorder and unintelligibility of politics. History, for Adams, was the attempt to understand politics in terms of broad, underlying themes such as the development of institutions or of national character; it was the discovery of orderly progression beneath the chaos of events. It need not, furthermore, be considered exclusively through moral spectacles; one might regard it with the detachment and impartiality of the scientist. Thus the study of American history became for him, at least partially, an effort to discover the inner meaning of what he had experienced in Washington, to locate the values hidden in that experience. When, for example, he returned in 1876 to the subject of the Constitution, his attitude toward it was significantly different from that expressed in his Washington pieces. In his review of Von Holst's *Constitutional and Political History of the United*

States, Adams sees the Constitution not as an embodiment of moral truth but as a "practical machine" for the creation of nationality. It is an agency resembling a natural "law" in its relentless, irreversible operation. The Constitution, in other words, had become for Adams part of a historical context, no longer an end in itself but pointing to ends beyond itself. Later still, when these deeper and more comprehensive ends eluded him, the mechanical metaphor of 1876 became a literal identification of history with the subject matter of the physical sciences. Adams concluded that only by penetrating like the scientist to the fundamental, material constituents of reality could the historian hope to learn the final and absolute truth contained in his materials. Thus Adams' quest for the meaning of history, touched off, though certainly not wholly sustained, by the failure of his youthful assumptions in Washington, ended in a kind of conversion of history into metaphysics in which the laws of matter ironically replaced the moral law transcending human legislation.

The second important effect of Adams' stay in Washington was the doubt engendered there of his adaptability to his own time. Every reader of the *Education* knows how troubled Adams was on this score; it became a major source of irony in the book written to expose what he called, with perverse insistence, his "failure." This sense of maladjustment goes back, I believe, to two things Adams learned in Washington: that a reasoned appeal to moral standards in politics is not necessarily persuasive—that government does, in fact, ignore moral responsibility—and that as a private individual, unallied with a party machine and armed only with the weapons of criticism, he was politically impotent. These two lessons, which are really opposite sides of the same coin, lie behind much of Adams' feeling of living in the wrong century. His consciousness of the ineffectuality of moral criticism combined with his inability to suppress his moral judgments produced the conviction that he was a member of an outmoded species, an anachronistic holdover from the eighteenth century of John and John Quincy Adams. At the same time, his disgust with party organizations, which were in his eyes the great source of corruption in American politics, and his impotence in the face of them, led to an identification of them with human nature and finally to despair at the prospect of reforming either politics or human nature. "Masses of men," he concluded in the *Education*, "invariably follow interests in deciding morals," which is to say that morality is irrelevant to politics. His own inherited moral code had been a "private and costly luxury," something that had gotten in the way of a true relation with his time and had prevented him from reacting "with vigor and economy" on the "lines of force" that attracted his world. Masses of men who followed their interests, on the other hand, seemed to him more and more as he grew older the blind, predestined agents of uncontrollable forces in history. The determinism of Adams' later years is remotely but unmistakably linked to the bafflement of his youthful hopes for reform and the forsaking of his social aspirations in response to the loss of his early faith.

One further observation is worth making with respect to the significance in Adams' career of the Washington episode. It has never been very clear why Adams, when he wrote as a professional historian, devoted himself exclusively to the period of Jeffersonian Republicanism. Superficially there would appear to be little reason for this choice. Adams was the great-grandson of a Federalist president and grandson of a president who was evicted from office by men who considered themselves the true heirs of Jefferson. He was a New Englander to the core and hence almost instinctively distrustful of the South and West where Jefferson had found his strongest support and where his theories had had the greatest influence. Why then should he have been interested in the Republican movement to the extent of fifteen years of labor, a nine-volume history, two biographies, and several volumes of edited papers?

The reasons are surely many and complicated, but a decisive one was the parallel Adams felt to exist between himself and the leaders of the first Republican party. As he saw them, the Republicans were the only true and distinctively American political idealists. They had tried to create, by means of concrete reforms and policies, a perfect governmental system and a new order of society in which the evils that had tormented human history would be ended and mankind set free to realize its highest natural capacities. In all of his books Adams gave the closest attention to these ideal hopes, and it is impossible not to feel in him a sympathetic identification with the men who held them. But in all of his books the same pattern of defeat and disillusionment is repeated, the chaos of events rises and sweeps away the frail structure of idealism; "circumstances" (as Adams called them in the *Life of Albert Gallatin*), in the form of intractable human nature and ineradicable social evil, triumph over "principles" helpless to control them. By the time he finished his *History*, Adams was certain that idealism in any form was illusory and doomed to such defeat.

It would be absurd, of course, to regard Adams as ever having been a Jeffersonian in politics, nor was he ever so wholehearted an idealist as he imagined the Republican leaders to have been, but the kinship he felt with them was based on a similarity of fate that was real—at least to his own mind. The whole of his youthful attitude toward politics rested on the belief that it was a struggle between right and wrong and that right must triumph. Washington and the subsequent breakdown of the reform movement convinced him that he had been mistaken, and the shock of his disappointment remained a powerful intellectual and emotional stimulus to the end of his life.

2

THE LIFE OF ALBERT GALLATIN

Aᴼᴳᴿ finishing in April and May of 1870 his two strongest pieces of criticism, "The New York Gold Conspiracy" and the second "Session," Henry Adams left Washington for a summer's visit to Europe. It was during this visit that he witnessed, amid the "rich and sensuous surroundings" of Bagni di Lucca, the horrible death of his sister from a tetanus infection, an event recorded in two or three of the most memorable pages of the *Education.* While at his sister's bedside, a letter reached him from President Charles W. Eliot of Harvard. It enclosed an offer of an assistant professorship in medieval history coupled with the editorship of the *North American Review.* Adams' reply was short and unambiguous. "The offer you make me is not only flattering but brilliant, yet I cannot accept it. Two years ago I should have hesitated long before deciding, but, having now chosen a career, I am determined to go on in it as far as it will lead me."

When he returned home, however, the "question of the professorship" was "sprung upon [him] again in a very troublesome way." Urged on all sides to accept, and evidently a good deal less sure of himself than he had thought, Adams vacillated for a week and then "yielded." In the long run, this was probably a fortunate accident; by the time he left Harvard Adams was a learned man and the foundation was laid for all his subsequent writing and speculation. But it is significant that his seven years at Harvard receive barely more than half a chapter in the *Education,* and that chapter is called "Failure." It seems clear that he remained permanently disappointed with himself for having given up the Washington experiment, although the *Education* places much of the blame upon President Grant. The removal to Harvard, after all, meant political defeat; it meant the abdication of the Adamses from national affairs. Despite his continued efforts on behalf of the Liberal Republicans, he knew he had surrendered a vital ambition, the ambition of power.

Nevertheless, he threw himself into teaching with great zest, and his early letters from Harvard reflect the same contentious and irreverent spirit as those from Washington. "There is a pleasing excitement," he told a friend, "in having to lecture tomorrow on a period of history which I have not even heard of till today." His energy was enormous: he devoured "three or four volumes of an evening," wrote letters in an endless stream, even in the midst of faculty meetings "while some thirty twaddlers are discussing questions of discipline around me," and managed almost singlehanded the affairs of the *North American.* In the classroom he disclaimed the pompous formalities of the professional academician. He provoked his students with questions, paradoxes, confessions of ignorance; it is reported that they sometimes laughed until their sides hurt. He began a graduate program in history, introducing the German seminar method, which led to his baking Harvard's first "batch of doctors of philosophy."

To complete the process of domestication begun when he left Washington for Cambridge, Henry Adams married, in June of 1872, Miss Marian Hooper of Boston. A few months before the wedding he described her in the following manner to his favorite correspondent, Charles Milnes Gaskell: "She is certainly not handsome; nor would she be quite called plain, I think. She is twenty-eight years old. She knows her own mind uncommon well. She does not talk *very* American. Her manners are quiet. She reads German—also Latin—also, I fear, a little Greek, but very little. . . . She dresses badly. She decidedly has humour and will appreciate *our* wit. She has enough money to be quite independent. She rules me as only American women rule men, and I cower before her. Lord! how she would lash me if she read the above description of her!"

Despite such evidence of *sang-froid,* Adams was deeply devoted to his wife and exceptionally attentive toward her. When she died by her own hand in 1885, he felt himself simply cut off from the world of the living and he never quite succeeded in re-establishing the connection again. His one consolation was that at least he "had got out of life all the pleasure it had to give."

Teaching and editing are repetitious work and eventually, to a mind of any strength, must prove a numbing routine. Adams at Harvard varied the routine by changing his subject. After two years of medieval history, he moved on to American history of the Colonial period, and finally to the early republic from 1789 to 1840. Now he became immersed in material that held his interest as no other could; he entered upon what was to become the major part of his life's work, an absorbing occupation of fifteen years. Simultaneously, the demands of teaching and the constrictions of Cambridge society irritated him increasingly. "I care a great deal," he wrote in 1875, "to prevent myself from becoming what of all things I despise, a Boston prig (the intellectual prig is the most odious of all), and so I yearn, at every instant, to get out of Massachusetts and come in contact with the wider life I always have found so much more to my taste."

His opportunity came early in 1877 when the son of Albert Gallatin, Jefferson's and Madison's Secretary of the Treasury, offered him Gallatin's papers and asked him to write a biography. Adams was immediately interested for the papers were a mine of unexplored material. They were all the pretext he needed for cutting his ties with Harvard; his university work, he had already decided, was "essentially done." In the summer of that year Adams and his wife "cut loose at once" from their academic life and moved to Washington. Adams felt renewed and buoyant. "The fact is," he said, "I gravitate to a capital by a primary law of nature. This is the only place in America where society amuses me, or where life offers variety. Here, too, I can fancy that we are of use in the world. . . ." He was now a professional historian, working for his own "original results." His name and friendships opened the vaults of the State Department to him; his circle of acquaintance once more included men of influence in worldly affairs, as well as scientists, artists, diplomats. He was forty years old, ripe for work, and in expansive spirits: "As I belong to the class of people who have great faith in this country and who believe that in another century it will be saying in its turn the last word of civilization, I enjoy the expectation of the coming day, and try to imagine that I am myself, with my fellow *gelehrte* here, the first faint rays of that great light which is to dazzle and set the world on fire hereafter."

✌ ✆

The Life of Albert Gallatin was published in 1879, the first fruit of Adams' researches into the Age of Jefferson. Much of the book is necessarily occupied with biographical details, but its central portion concerning Gallatin's years in Congress and the Treasury, from 1795 to 1813, is given coherence and meaning by the theme of the rise and fall of democratic idealism. The treatment of this theme is especially interesting because the *Life of Gallatin* is the first of a connected series of books all dealing with Jeffersonian Republicanism, which was the great vehicle, as Adams saw it, of the democratic movement in the United States. *Gallatin* broaches the subject, exposes Adams' still somewhat tentative thoughts about it, and indicates the direction for its later development in his work. Its indications, furthermore, are excellent guides to that development, for the pattern of ideas adumbrated in this book in connection with the theme of democracy remains in all essentials the permanent one.

The core of democratic idealism in all of Adams' historical work is the belief in human perfectibility. Not until the *History*, however, was he able to give this belief the treatment it deserved; in *Gallatin* he seems not quite convinced of its importance as a motive in American history. Still, one of his most frequent and significant observations concerning the Republicans is that they possessed what in one place is

WINGATE COLLEGE LIBRARY
WINGATE, N. C.

called a "sublime confidence in human nature." What this confidence implied is quite vague, yet one may deduce at least a formulable concept of its meaning from hints dropped now and then by Adams in some of his more reflective passages. For instance, in explaining Gallatin's rash and headlong departure from Geneva at the age of nineteen, Adams places chief responsibility on the "intellectual movement" of his time and place; the "clear-headed, sober-minded, practical Genevan" was "affiliated with a knot of young men who, if not quite followers of Rousseau, were still essentially visionaries. . . . They believed in human nature, and believed that human nature when free from social trammels would display nobler qualities and achieve vaster results, not merely in the physical but also in the moral world." On a similar note, Adams later says of Gallatin that, "loathing the violence, the extravagance, the corruption of Europe, he clung with what in a less calm mind would seem passionate vehemence to the ideal he had formed of a great and pure society in the New World, which was to offer to the human race the first example of man in his best condition, free from all the evils which infected Europe, and intent only on his own improvement."

Adams' language is revealing, too, in his attempts to state in general terms the final objects of the Republican administrations:

> To make one comprehensive, permanent provision for the moral and economical development of the people, to mark out the path of progress with precision and to enter upon it at least so far as to make subsequent advance easy and certain . . .

> It was not a mere departmental reform or a mere treasury administration that Mr. Gallatin undertook; it was a theory of democratic government which he and his associates attempted to reduce to practice. . . . As their scheme existed in the minds of Mr. Jefferson, Mr. Gallatin, and Mr. Madison, it was broad as society itself, and aimed at providing for and guiding the moral and material development of a new era,—a fresh race of men.

"This," Adams remarks, just after the first of these comments, "was the highest statesmanship, the broadest practical philanthropy."

The gist of the foregoing extracts may be paraphrased thus: democracy starts with a faith in the innate capacity of human beings, when free of social restraint and encouraged by a democratic social order, to progress both morally and materially toward an ideal secular condition, a state of human perfection. This formula is not a very concrete one, but even as an abstraction its importance to Adams' mind cannot be exaggerated. It profoundly illuminates his attitude toward history, the subject that was to provide so much food for his later thought. With respect to Republicanism, two aspects of the formula are particularly significant. First, according to it democracy posits a final goal of human development; perpetual change, even in the direction of improvement, without such a final goal would imply some ineradicable flaw in human nature and therefore some permanent condition of evil in the world. In this sense, the Republicans were for Adams true idealists; the end that could alone justify their "sublime confidence in human nature" was some sort of perfection, an absolute and unchangeable good. Second, as idealists of this order, Adams' Republicans were necessarily imbued with a strong sense of purposiveness, both in their own lives and in the movement of history as a whole. History took on meaning for them either as progress or the delay of progress toward the ideal goal. Each man, too, saw his own life and deeds as contributing to progress, and found in the degree of his contribution a measure of his success. The meaning of a life like Gallatin's was thus clearly defined as the pursuit of an ideal end, namely that "great and pure society in the New World, which was to offer to the human race the first example of man in his best condition."

When one recognizes the original impulse of Republicanism for what it was, the political narrative of Adams' book acquires a depth, and even a symbolic value, that are not perceptible at first glance. These historical actors, we realize, played for the biggest possible stakes; their whole beings and the being of a nation were involved: Mr. Jefferson "would rather have let the world perish than that this principle . . . should fail." And as idealists they dramatize in their way a permanent human theme; each act and gesture is given by its context something of universality, an interest wider than the limits of its own particular historical applicability. From this point of view, Republican ideology and statesmanship transcend party programs and ultimately even national programs. They are embodiments of a wish to achieve the ideal; the democratic system is a means of concretizing the ideal. Its absolute success would mean the inauguration of "a new era,—a fresh race of men."

How, then, did the Republicans go about trying to realize in specific political measures their dream of transforming society? Essentially, as Adams saw it, they put their faith in governmental limitation, in the attempt to curb and check that power which in all previous ages of the world had been used to oppress men and block the progress of society. With a strength and distinctness of belief that amounted practically to reinvention, the Republicans took over the old maxim which said (in Gallatin's phrasing) "our government always fails by doing or attempting to do and to govern too much, and . . . things never go better than when we are doing very little."

But Gallatin's energies were chiefly devoted to matters of finance, and it is with the financial policies of the first three Republican administrations that the central portion of Adams' book is principally concerned. Adams sees Gallatin as the mainspring of Republican

"practical statesmanship," the man who gave tangible economic form
to Jefferson's "philanthropic and humanitarian doctrines." Gallatin's
role, Adams thinks, was comparable to Hamilton's, whose "vigor and
capacity of . . . mind are seen at their best . . . in the mass and
variety of legislation and organization which characterized the first
Administration of Washington, and which were permeated and controlled by Hamilton's spirit. . . . What Hamilton was to Washington,
Gallatin was to Jefferson. . . ."

In tracing the development of Gallatin's financial policy, therefore,
we must necessarily be at the very center of the Republicans' effort to
capture and institutionalize their ideal. "In so far as Mr. Jefferson's
Administration represented a change of system, its positive characteristics," says Adams, "were financial." He then summarizes them:

> . . . that America, standing outside the political movement of Eu-
> rope, could afford to follow a political development of her own; that
> she might safely disregard remote dangers; that her armaments might
> be reduced to a point little above mere police necessities; that she
> might rely on natural self-interest for her foreign commerce; that she
> might depend on average common sense for her internal prosperity and
> order; and that her capital was safest in the hands of her own citizens.
> To establish these doctrines beyond the chance of overthrow was to
> make democratic government a success. . . .

> In this political scheme . . . everything was made to depend upon
> financial management, and, since the temptation to borrow money was
> the great danger, payment of the debt was the great dogma of the
> Democratic principle.

With the last sentence Adams provides a key to his subsequent history of Republicanism and of Gallatin's leadership in it. The "everything" that depended on financial management included not only the
structure of democratic government but the ideal of democratic aspiration as well, the incomparably valuable goal of "a new era,—a fresh
race of men." The success or failure of the policy of avoidance and
payment of debt is thus made by Adams to bear the chief burden of
responsibility for Republican success or failure as a whole. In reading
the long chapter on Gallatin's Treasury years, therefore, our attention
is directed by the author to those sections dealing with this policy.

The reasons for the Republican abhorrence of national debt are not
hard to find. National debt was, in the first place, a centralizing influence, a "means of consolidating divergent local interests." By bor-
rowing from its own citizens, thought the Republicans, a government
diverts wealth from its proper employments which are private capital
investment or direct improvement of the sources of wealth such as
farms, stock, and factories. Furthermore, control by the government
of large amounts of borrowed money inevitably means increased power.

Citizens are made dependent on the government's ability to repay; officials acquire undue influence through their management of funds; opportunities for extravagance, waste, corruption, political pressure, become more and more available and tempting. Most important of all, the necessity to keep up continual payments on the interest of debt ingrains the habit of taxation, a taxation that always falls most heavily on small farmers, businessmen, and laborers. And finally, debtlessness was a moral virtue for the Republicans. A government that could not live within its income was incapable of providing for the moral development of a fresh race of men.

Thus everything depended upon financial management and payment of the national debt. What success did the Republicans achieve in this field of policy? Before he offers at length the answer to this question, Adams gives one small clue that foretells the outcome of Republican ambition quite plainly. In order to succeed, the Republicans needed peace; without it their control of the government would become useless for the establishment of a democratic system. "To use . . . Mr. Gallatin's own words . . . : 'No nation can, any more than any individual, pay its debts unless its annual receipts exceed its expenditures, and the two necessary ingredients for that purpose . . . are frugality and peace.'" War means an automatic and usually exorbitant increase in expenditures, with its accompanying evils of taxation, waste, and, in a poor country, declining income and productivity. War would shatter the Republican dream by simply wiping out whatever progress had been made toward the purification of society. In 1812, of course, the war which had long been threatening broke out between the United States and Great Britain; in 1813 Mr. Gallatin resigned as Secretary of the Treasury. It was, to use one of Adams' many similar expressions, "the ultimate shipwreck."

It is unnecessary to follow in detail the sequence of events that led to this shipwreck, but it is of utmost importance to understand that, for Adams, it meant the failure of Republican policy and, by implication, the defeat of democratic idealism. From 1808 on, as relations between the United States and Britain and France grew more critical, Gallatin and his associates found themselves compelled to abandon one after another the old Republican principles by which they had hoped to remake society. Instead of strict neutrality based on impartial commerce with all of Europe, they were forced to engage in commercial warfare; instead of reliance on private interest in trade, they were forced to make government its arbiter and suppressor; instead of tax reduction, the Republicans were forced to impose a heavier burden of taxation on the American people than had ever been known before. Gallatin himself had the grim duty of drawing up a program of war taxes and of outlining a scheme whereby the government might borrow the $50,000,000 estimated to be necessary for prosecuting the war.

After having reduced the national debt by over $42,000,000 in ten years, he saw it increased by $78,000,000 in two and a half years, while the resources of the treasury, succumbing not only to need but to the wartime evils of waste and extravagance, were exhausted.

These figures alone are enough to tell the fate of "the great dogma of the Democratic principle." The other cardinal rule of Republicanism, the limitation of governmental authority and especially that of the executive, suffered, Adams thought, a comparable defeat. Ironically, this resulted in the main from an attempt to stick rigidly by democratic theory, and the irony was not lost upon Adams. In 1807 when the British ministry announced its Orders in Council which clamped tight restrictions on all neutral shipping, the Jefferson administration retaliated with its famous Embargo Act. The British purpose, as Adams puts it, was to crush "the commercial growth of America" by making its trade entirely dependent upon Britain's interest. The American purpose was to avoid either submission or war, to adhere, despite all provocation, to the policy of isolation and neutrality in the struggle between England and France. Jefferson was convinced that shutting off American trade would make both combatants realize how valuable it was, and would lead ultimately to the peaceable restoration of American rights. To satisfy the national interest without war—this was Jefferson's intention, the heart of his foreign policy, and the reason why he clung so obstinately to the Embargo even in the face of its palpable ineffectuality and the ever-mounting national hostility against it.

But in order for the Embargo to have any chance of success, it had to be enforced against enterprising American shippers willing to do business on British terms. The moral difficulty this problem caused Jefferson's administration is expatiated on at length by Adams, and his remarks show the peculiar concern he felt about the idealism underlying Republican motives. To stop commerce was, in effect, to stop "the whole action and industry of all the great cities and much of the rural population," and required "no ordinary grant of powers."

Thus the astonishing spectacle was presented of Mr. Jefferson, Mr. Madison, and Mr. Gallatin, the apostles of strict construction, of narrow grants, the men who of all others were the incarnation of that theory which represented mankind as too much governed, and who, according to Mr. Jefferson, would have had government occupy itself exclusively with foreign affairs and leave the individual absolutely alone to manage his own concerns in his own way,—of these men demanding, obtaining, and using powers practically unlimited so far as private property was concerned; powers in comparison with which the alien and sedition laws were narrow and jealous in their grants; powers which placed the fortunes of at least half the community directly under their control; which made them no more nor less than despots. . . .

To anyone acquainted with the *Education* a certain characteristic Adamsian manner is recognizable in this passage. The tone of exaggeration, the deliberate and heightened contrasts, tell as much, if not more than, the explicit statements. They locate Adams' feelings; they draw his emphasis away from any rational justification of the Republicans' actions and place it on the gap between their professed beliefs and their actual deeds. The effect of the passage is to bring home sharply the author's consciousness of the failure of Republican idealism in the cold war of 1807–1812.

Indeed, the Embargo figures as a major turning point in Republican fortunes, and, judging by his use of it in all three of the historical works, it was a symbolic event of the first importance to Adams' mind. The reason for this is clearly suggested by the quotation in the preceding paragraph. That the Republicans should themselves have somehow been responsible for their own failure; that men of the highest principle and noblest aim, men like Jefferson, Madison, and Gallatin, should have contributed to the defeat of their own high principles and noble aims—all this struck Adams as the height of historical irony. He could not resist dwelling on the contradictions to which the Republicans fell victim; his tone is frequently one of shock or incredulity, like a man telling himself that what he sees with his own eyes is true though he can hardly bring himself to believe it or, more precisely, accept it. When, for example, Adams comes to speak of the Enforcement Act of 1808, a bill designed at Gallatin's request to put more effective teeth in the Embargo, he calls it "a terrible measure, and in comparison with its sweeping grants of arbitrary power, all previous enactments of the United States Congress sank into comparative insignificance. How it could be defended under any conceivable theory of the Republican party, and how it could receive the support of any Republican whose memory extended ten years back, are questions which would be difficult to answer if the Annals of Congress were not at hand to explain." The answer that Adams proceeds in the next sentence to draw from the Annals of Congress summarizes the almost outrageous state of contradiction into which Republicanism had fallen. "The two parties had completely changed their position, and while the Republicans stood on the ground once occupied by the Federalists, the Federalists were seeking safety under the States' rights doctrines formerly avowed by the Virginia and Kentucky Republicans."

Naturally, such a blatant reversal, such an unbridgeable chasm between profession and act, require explanation. The historian must ask of the facts: What forces were capable of effecting such an irony? In what way and to what extent were the Republicans responsible for their own downfall? These questions open up problems of great importance for Adams and for the student of his mind. They lead Adams, in the first place, toward a theory of history and, in the second, toward

a critique of Republicanism. If the Republicans were forced, against
their will, to stand on the ground once occupied by the Federalists,
there must have been something in the nature of the events with
which they had to cope that was powerful enough to drive them on to
Federalist ground. And must not their own policies, which had helped
to shape those events, have been, at least in part, to blame for the
effects they had produced? In the *Life of Albert Gallatin* Adams re-
sorts to fairly tentative and unsatisfactory solutions to both these
problems. That is to say, his theory of history is vague, and his critique
of Republicanism is neither very original nor very deeply influenced
by the theory of history on which ultimately it must depend. Nevertheless, the solutions put forth in *Gallatin* demand careful attention.

So far as the author of *Gallatin* is concerned, the historical truth
that seems to emerge universally from the facts of history is that "circumstances must by their nature be stronger and more permanent than
men." These are the words, at any rate, with which Adams tries to
explain the irony of Republicans turned "despots." Circumstances control men; the "brutal directness with which Mr. Canning kicked
Mr. Jefferson's diplomacy out of his path" and went about his policy
of "crushing the commercial growth of America,"—these circumstances
forced the Embargo; the Embargo in its turn created circumstances
that forced extension of the government's powers; everywhere circumstances proved stronger and more permanent than men, no matter
how pure their motives. "Brought at last face to face with this new
political fact which gave the lie to all his theories and hopes, even the
sanguine and supple Jefferson felt the solid earth reel under him. . . ."

That circumstances should show themselves to be so powerful—
powerful enough to overthrow their whole system—was obviously not
what the Republicans had expected. On the contrary, their confidence
in human nature and in the perfect desirability of their ideal ends
had led them to expect that principles would govern circumstances.
The whole difference between them and the Federalists is at one point
stated by Adams to be nothing other than that the Republicans believed "government must be ruled by principles; to which the Federalists answered that government must be ruled by circumstances."
Only with this sentence in mind do we appreciate the full savor of the
irony by which "the Republicans stood on the ground once occupied
by the Federalists."

Circumstances, then, appear to be those things outside of men in
the world which resist their control and, in the end, outlast them.
Events, conditions, other men, whatever asserts its independence of
the human will and is capable of asserting its own claims upon it—
these, for Adams, constitute an intractable reality "stronger and more
permanent" than idealism. To recognize this inevitably means to
abandon, or "outgrow," idealism. Gallatin, whom Adams admired un-

reservedly—"I am more than ever convinced that for combination of ability, integrity, knowledge, unselfishness, and social fitness Mr. Gallatin has no equal. He was the most fully and perfectly equipped statesman we can show"—Gallatin himself outgrew "the Jeffersonian dogmas." When he buckled down to enforce the Embargo, "He knew . . . how far he had drifted from his true course, and how arbitrary, odious, and dangerous was the course he had to pursue; but he at least now learned to recognize in the fullest extent the omnipotence of circumstance. He had no longer a principle to guide him. Except, somewhere far in the background, a general theory that peace was better than war, not a shred was left of Republican principles. Facts, not theories, were all that survived. . . ."

Some more light can be thrown on the "omnipotence of circumstance" if we examine further its relation to idealism. What is it about idealism that makes it so weak at the hands of facts? Why did "the Jeffersonian dogmas" have to be outgrown? Adams has one ready answer to these questions:

> The weak point of what may be called the Jeffersonian system lay in its rigidity of rule. That system was, it must be confessed, a system of doctrinaires, and had the virtues and faults of *a priori* reasoning. Far in advance, as it was, of any other political effort of its time, and representing, as it doubtless did, all that was most philanthropic and all that most boldly appealed to the best instincts of mankind, it made too little allowance for human passions and vices; it relied too absolutely on the power of interest and reason as opposed to prejudice and habit; it proclaimed too openly to the world that the sword was not one of its arguments, and that peace was essential to its existence.

And so, in effect, it invited the war that destroyed it.

Republicanism, as Adams saw it, confronted experience with *a priori* reasoning, with theories and principles and all the assorted paraphernalia of idealism, only to discover that the facts were stronger and more permanent. What is more, the rigidity imposed upon the Republicans by their own previous decisions enhanced the destructive power of the facts. Whereas Gallatin, soon after the passage of the Embargo Act, came to prefer war as an alternative to stagnation, Jefferson and the Congress dominated by his spirit clung to the Embargo despite growing economic ruin, internal disorganization, and crumbling morale—all of which only encouraged British arrogance and made the American task harder when war finally did come. The old Federalist policy might, Adams hints, have been the only one able to prevent a war after all: naval armaments rather than payment of the debt; alliance with England rather than neutrality; the rule, in other words, of circumstances rather than principle.

But at bottom the chief flaw in the Republican attitude was precisely that which gave it its philanthropic mission and boldness of appeal.

The "sublime confidence in human nature," from which the Republicans drew strength to oppose the Federalist presidents and to seize national power, failed in its justification. Despite eight quiet years of Republican government, the "passions and vices" of men remained just as strong as they had ever been; moral progress had not been accomplished. This failure struck at the root of democratic idealism and, in fact, killed it. From the period of the war onward, although the Republican party remained active and, in some respects, doctrinaire, it was no longer, according to Adams, a party of idealism but merely a party (so far as distinctions still held in the "era of good feelings") with its own view of the omnipotent circumstances. The best of the Republican leaders realized their mistake and accepted its consequences as philosophically as they could. Gallatin wrote to an old friend in 1825, "As to the world, I have been, like you, disappointed in the estimate I had formed of the virtue of mankind and of its influence over others. Every day's experience convinces us that most unprincipled men are often most successful." Nevertheless, he said, "I have had so much greater share of all that appears desirable than I had any right to expect, that I have none to complain," and he continued to devote himself for the rest of his life to the cause of virtue and of knowledge, taking a much more patient view, we must suppose, of human progress than was conceivable in his youth.

To Adams' eyes, Gallatin is something of a tragic hero in the drama of Republicanism's rise and fall. Having suffered defeat, a defeat caused in part by his own best intentions, he retained his integrity of character, his unselfishness of spirit, while being able at the same time to acknowledge the truth of what had passed. Although "he had outgrown the convictions which had made his strength; he had not, indeed, lost confidence in himself, for, throughout all his trials and disappointments, the tone of his mind had remained as pure as when he began life, and he had never forfeited his self-respect. . . ." Unlike Jefferson, for example, he was capable of rising to a new level of insight into political affairs, bleak as it must have been for him. "His statesmanship [i.e., postwar diplomacy] had become, what practical statesmanship always has and must become, a mere struggle to deal with concrete fact at the cost of philosophic and *a priori* principles." He thus managed to turn defeat into a triumph of personal integrity.

Jefferson does not come off so well, although it is hard to make a comparison since he drops out of the book almost completely after 1809. On the whole, Adams' attitude toward Jefferson is one of respect tinged with irony, an irony, however, not marked by the bitterness which is noticeable in *John Randolph*. So far as American history is concerned, Adams is willing to accord Jefferson a very high place indeed, one at the side of George Washington: "Washington and Jefferson doubtless stand pre-eminent as the representatives of what is best in our national character or its aspirations. . . ." And whenever the philanthropic and humanitarian aspects of Republicanism are mentioned, they are invariably linked with Jefferson's name. He was the arch-idealist, the most fervent believer in human nature, the most ardent aspirer to human progress and perfection. But, as might be expected, he suffered more seriously than anyone else from the faults of his virtues. If "the Jeffersonian system . . . was . . . a system of doctrinaires," Jefferson was, in Adams' eyes, the most doctrinaire of the lot, the most stubborn to yield up principle no matter how disastrous the effects of his stubbornness might be. He had not Gallatin's ability to rise above disappointment, to absorb painful knowledge. When the Republicans were brought face to face with the breakdown of the Embargo and the triumph of circumstances over idealism, Jefferson's resiliency was shattered, "and his courage fled; it was long before he recovered his old confidence, and he never could speak of the embargo and the last years of his Presidency without showing traces of the mental shock he had suffered." However, Jefferson is on the whole treated by Adams with respect. In the *Life of Gallatin* he is seen primarily as the spiritual leader of Republican idealism, essentially a high-minded, generous, and visionary man, whose impact on American history has been profound and long lasting. "Except those theories of government which are popularly represented by the names of Hamilton and Jefferson, no solution of the great problems of American politics has ever been offered to the American people. Since the day when foreign violence and domestic faction prostrated Mr. Gallatin and his two friends, no statesman has ever appeared with the strength to bend their bow,—to finish their uncompleted task."

◄◊ ◊►

Three basic facts of vital significance to the understanding of Henry Adams' mind are revealed by the *Life of Albert Gallatin*. The first is that he conceived of Republicanism as a system designed to realize an ideal of human perfection. Given such a conception, the lives of all those involved in the Republican movement were necessarily seen by him in a certain way, namely as deriving their meaning from the effort to achieve the ideal. The second basic fact is that the writing of biography meant to Adams primarily a study of the pursuit of ideal ends. Gallatin's life, insofar as it discloses a form to the biographer, is nothing else than just such a pursuit. The third fact we learn from this book is that Republicanism did not succeed in establishing its ideal society; Gallatin's life was a pursuit that terminated in failure. The failure of Gallatin portends quite definitely the failure Henry Adams attributed to himself in his autobiography, and the context of Gallatin's failure—the context of democratic idealism—helps suggest a way of interpreting Adams' failure.

3

~ DEMOCRACY

IN THE early part of 1879, soon after Adams had finished the *Life of Gallatin* and had begun research for his *History of the United States,* Adams wrote his first work of fiction: *Democracy,* subtitled *An American Novel.* It is steeped in the same current of thought that flows through the historical works and has much to reveal about Adams' state of mind during the period of their composition. Indeed, it seems that by the act of putting aside history and creating a set of symbolic personalities and events, Adams was liberated to discover, or at least to express, some of his most deeply felt convictions.

This liberation was undoubtedly aided by the fact that the book was published anonymously, its authorship a close secret until 1909 and not widely known until 1920. An obvious reason for anonymity was that *Democracy* reflected Adams' views of several quite recognizable people, among whom the best known was Senator James G. Blaine. Blaine, the model for Senator Ratcliffe of the novel, was then at the peak of his congressional career; he was soon to become Secretary of State and, in 1884, the Republican party's nominee for president. Withal, he was one of the most notoriously equivocal personages, morally speaking, of the Gilded Age. To Adams he was a veritable *bête noire,* someone to be shunned politically and ignored socially, even at the cost of considerable inconvenience or embarrassment. That Blaine, as well as the rest of the world, knew of his role in *Democracy* is evidenced by the public cut he administered to Clarence King, Adams' close friend and one of those (Mrs. Adams was another) reputed to be the novel's author.

The anonymity of *Democracy* is also connected with the Puritanism so strongly ingrained in Adams' character. To his mind the writing of novels must have stood with respect to the writing of history much as Quincy, in the famous antithesis of the *Education,* stood with respect to Boston. Whereas Boston was "restraint, law, unity," Quincy, the home of summer, was "liberty, diversity, outlawry." For Adams the novel was personal as against the impersonality of history; it provided an escape from the historian's responsibility to fact and universal truth. The novel was a product of a different self from the one that wrote history, a self that might only be indulged in secret and could not be allowed to mar the image of the professional historian. The guilt associated with the expression of this other self, and the repression that was manifested in anonymity, evoked a curious schizophrenia in Adams with regard to authorship. "My ideal of authorship," he once said, "would be to have a famous *double* with another name, to wear what honors I could win. How I should enjoy upsetting him at last by publishing a low and shameless essay with smutty woodcuts in his name!" The alternative to such a fantasy was anonymity and, after the publication of *Esther*, which was attended by the most painful guilt for its revelation of intimacy, anonymity sank into silence. Except for the *History* and a very few other professional or theoretical pieces, Adams never again wrote for the general public.

Beyond its importance within the framework of Adams' literary development, *Democracy*'s claim to consideration is supported by its own literary merit, its independent quality as a novel. Although it is partially true that, as R. P. Blackmur has said, Adams "lacked the native gift of the story-teller,"[1] still the subject of *Democracy* is a difficult one, its interest in human beings is serious, and its structural craft, though occasionally mechanical or stiff, is adequate to its intention. Instead of exhaustiveness it aims for verbal dexterity, a dry, witty economy that compresses its material and communicates insight in the form of epithet. Its mode of complexity, as therefore might be expected, is paradox or, more generally, an irony that plays over much of its surface, lighting up unexpressed motive, thought, or desire. A measure of Adams' success, in fact, is the extent to which his wit enlivens and deepens the book without diminishing its seriousness or reducing the stature of its heroes and their moral plight.

There are two levels of meaning in *Democracy,* one defined by its theme or conscious intention, the other by its motives which are implicit in structure and which relate the novel to the primary sources of all of Adams' work. As far as its theme is concerned, *Democracy* is an analysis of political values and organization in the United States. It is an exposition, in concrete terms, of the meaning of contemporary American "democracy." It begins with Mrs. Madeline Lee's intention "to see with her own eyes the action of primary forces; to touch with her own hand the massive machinery of society; to measure with her own mind the capacity of the motive power. She was bent upon getting to the heart of the great American mystery of democracy and government." It ends with her solution of the mystery by means of her insight into Senator Ratcliffe's character and her rejection of his marriage proposal. The line between these two points is clear and distinct.

---

[1] "The Novels of Henry Adams," *Sewanee Review,* LI (1943), 281–304.

After Mrs. Lee has set her sights on the "great American mystery of democracy and government," it is natural that she should recognize in Senator Ratcliffe, the Prairie Giant from Peonia, Illinois, the key to her mystery. "To her eyes he was the high-priest of American politics; he was charged with the meaning of the mysteries, the clue to political hieroglyphics. Through him she hoped to sound the depths of statesmanship and to bring up from its oozy bed that pearl of which she was in search; the mysterious gem which must lie hidden somewhere in politics. She wanted to understand this man; to turn him inside out. . . . If there was good or bad in him she meant to find its meaning." This puts the Senator in a crucial position. He is the chief embodiment of political significance, the one figure in whom the author's conscious ideas about democracy must be fully represented.

The portrayal of Senator Ratcliffe exhibits an egotism so impermeable and an amorality so unconscious and pervasive as ultimately to call forth violence on the part of both the heroine and the author as the only way of dealing with it. From the moment Mrs. Lee lands him, like a "huge, two-hundred-pound salmon," with a bait of absolutely shameless flattery, to the hour of his marriage proposal, "the most unsentimental and businesslike" she had ever heard, the Senator plays all the stops of an intense and brutal selfishness. He is shown twisting, with equal relish, both the President of the United States and Mrs. Madeline Lee about his finger; he lies profusely, mouths pious hypocrisies incessantly, and is constantly engaged in the most underhanded political manipulation while wearing the mantle of a martyred son of the prairie, one of nature's noblemen. He is, in fact, a consummate actor of whatever role accords best with the demands of his ego and the moral or intellectual weakness of his victims; ultimately he is without real identity, a naked will operating under conditions of moral lunacy.

This crushing knowledge comes to Mrs. Lee, although she had long been half aware of it, under the pressure created by Ratcliffe's proposal and Carrington's letter disclosing the Senator's guilt as a bribetaker. As she listens to Ratcliffe try to justify his taking of the bribe as an act of loyalty to his party—"a great political party which I looked upon as identical with the nation"—it seems to her that "not until this moment had she really felt as though she had got to the heart of politics, so that she could, like a physician with his stethoscope, measure the organic disease." The disease she measures is diagnosed as a total "atrophy of the moral senses."

The audacity of the man [in disclaiming moral responsibility for his acts and throwing it entirely upon "the party"] would have seemed sublime if she had felt sure that he knew the difference between good and evil, between a lie and the truth; but the more she saw of him, the surer she was that his courage was mere moral paralysis, and that he talked about virtue and vice as a man who is color-blind talks about red and green; he did not see them as she saw them; if left to choose for himself he would have nothing to guide him.

The chaos of Senator Ratcliffe's moral condition is the key to "the great American mystery of democracy and government." The mystery shrouds nothing but a senseless clash of egos, a clash whose political significance is the negation of any impersonal value in democracy. To Mrs. Lee the final truth about democracy is that "it was nothing more than government of any other kind," a mere struggle to acquire power for its own sake. In a democracy, just as in government of any other kind, "the mere possession of power could convert the shadow of a hobby-horse existing only in the brain of a foolish country farmer, into a lurid nightmare that convulsed the sleep of nations," and no impersonal principle, no end beyond the exercise of power itself, could control that power to higher and better uses. The conclusion Mrs. Lee arrives at, hand in hand with her creator, is that democracy has no special value as a system of government and no meaning as an ideal. In the terminating action of the book she bitterly rejects Ratcliffe's effort to draw her by marriage into the world of democratic government. And when Ratcliffe leaves the scene of this rejection, Adams cannot resist further chastising him through the agency of old Baron Jacobi who administers a sound caning. Perhaps, all in all, Jacobi has the last word in more than one way. His judgment, uttered early in the book, rings like an absolute doom over all its pages:

In all my experience I have found no society which has had elements of corruption like the United States. The children in the street are corrupt, and know how to cheat me. The cities are all corrupt, and also the towns and the counties and the States' legislatures and the judges. Everywhere men betray trusts both public and private, steal money, run away with public funds. . . . I do much regret that I have not yet one hundred years to live. If I could then come back to this city, I should find myself very content. . . . I am always content where there is much corruption, and *ma parole d'honneur!* . . . the United States will then be more corrupt than Rome under Caligula; more corrupt than the Church under Leo X; more corrupt than France under the Regent!

The critique of American democracy voiced in this novel stems directly from Adams' belief, expressed in the *Life of Gallatin,* that democratic idealism had failed with the collapse of the Jeffersonian system of government. After the deluge, Ratcliffe is all that remains. He is implicit in the Federalist notion that government should be ruled by circumstances rather than by principles. Ratcliffe himself is always appealing to circumstances, to the perilous state of the union, to the imperfection of public morality, to the necessities of party survival, to whatever will excuse his temporary acquiescence in evil. He is the dead end to which American politics has come since the triumph of circumstances over Republican confidence in human nature.

᠊᠊᠊᠊ ᠊᠊᠊᠊

To this dead end Adams brings the heroine of his novel in her search for the meaning of democracy. But if we understand what her arrival there signifies politically, we may still inquire: what does her search itself mean? What has motivated it, and what reasons justify its conclusion? What are the grounds of Mrs. Lee's rejection of democracy in the person of Senator Ratcliffe, and where does this decision leave her? To answer these questions, which lead to the motives in Adams that shaped the book and caused its writing, it is necessary to examine the character of Mrs. Lee and the movement of her thought and action in their full development.

Mrs. Lee arrives in Washington with more on her mind than simply a desire to find out the truth about democracy. She is a woman fleeing from a ruined and empty life, from the ennui bred of triviality and aimlessness. Adams tells us that five years before, she lost in one week her husband and her child, an experience that at first made her almost mad with grief and longing for death, and in the end turned her into a stoic "fairly hardened to insensibility" by the exhaustion of her former life. " 'To lose a husband and a baby,' said she, 'and keep one's courage and reason, one must become very hard or very soft. I am now pure steel. You may beat my heart with a trip-hammer and it will beat the trip-hammer back again.' "

At the same time that she has become very hard, Mrs. Lee has also become very critical. The once "rather fast" and stylish New York girl has been transformed by her suffering into a cool observer and judge of the life around her; "she had become serious." The social life and organized philanthropy of New York's *haut monde* into which she threw herself after her calamity have proved incapable of sustaining her seriousness. Society is a dreary round of complacent stockbrokers seasoned with an occasional "transcendental commission-merchant." Philanthropy only serves to "increase and perpetuate the same kind of human nature which was her great grievance." Even "philosophy in the original German" is "so much culture [that leads] to nothing. . . ." Life seems to Mrs. Lee "a wilderness of men and women as monotonous as the brown stone houses they [live] in."

At the outset of the novel, then, Mrs. Lee is undergoing, behind her genteel exterior, a crisis of the spirit brought on by the apparent meaninglessness of her life and the lives around her. Her personal tragedy has forced a new consciousness upon her, a standard by which she cannot help measuring the insignificance of society's common occupations. At the same time it has filled her with the need to find something not insignificant, something worthy of her seriousness and intelligence to which she can devote her remaining energies. She has had all her naïve egotism, like that which still belongs to her sister Sybil Ross, burned out of her. Instead, there is in her a great untapped capacity for self-sacrifice, a desire to give herself up to whatever can make a rightful claim upon her sense of duty. In short, she is a woman in search of a meaning for her life, "eating her heart out because she could find no one object worth a sacrifice." This is the true reason behind her flight from New York to Washington. Democracy represents the possibility of meaning, of holding out to her an "object worth a sacrifice." Only in this perspective can her Washington adventures be rightly understood.

There is, however, another element of her nature that is called into play by Mrs. Lee's quest for an object worthy of sacrifice. The other side of her refusal to let life dribble away in trivialities is an ambition to use it importantly, perhaps nobly, at least effectively. She is drawn to Washington because, whatever else it may be, it is important; decisions are made there that affect the lives of millions and the course of history itself. She is drawn, as Adams himself inescapably was, to the source of power. "What she wished to see, she thought, was the clash of interests, the interests of forty millions of people and a whole continent, centering at Washington; guided, restrained, controlled, or unrestrained and uncontrollable, by men of ordinary mould; the tremendous forces of government, and the machinery of society, at work. What she wanted, was POWER." To want power is ambition; yet such ambition need not, Mrs. Lee feels, be merely egoistic. Power itself, power in capital letters, can be used impersonally, in the service of good. But can it? Neither the author nor Mrs. Lee is quite sure for a long time whether or not "the human interest of politics was after all what really attracted her, and, however strongly she might deny it, the passion for exercising power, for its own sake, might dazzle and mislead a woman who had exhausted all the ordinary feminine resources." This uncertainty of motive is crucial, for precisely because of it Mrs. Lee is vulnerable to the besiegement of Senator Ratcliffe.

The Senator employs, in his wooing of Mrs. Lee, what Carrington mentally calls "his usual theory of political corruption as applied to feminine weaknesses." That is, he assumes that power for its own sake *must* be the end of Mrs. Lee's ambition, even though she insists that what she really wants is good for its own sake. He therefore sets about to confuse the moral issues connected with the exercise of power, while always subtly extending to her the opportunity to taste power through her influence over him. His most devilish technique is to involve her in his moral decisions, thus making her to some extent responsible for them. He tells her of his fixing an Illinois election count, and she barely gags over this when he, with disarming frankness, justifies his action as sanctioned by the unimpeachable end of preserving the Union. He seeks her advice when the wicked new President invites him into the Cabinet, painting himself as a sacrificial lamb being led to the slaughter by his own unselfish patriotism. In each case he disguises the true situation, shielding Mrs. Lee from any hint which might suggest that the only thing uniting his numerous base acts for noble ends has been the chance they afforded for augmenting his power and prestige. By continually representing politics as a hell of iniquity and himself as one of nature's noblemen, Ratcliffe aims to identify in Mrs. Lee's mind his own love of power and her higher moral aspirations. In this way he expects that she will gradually be drawn into his hypocrisy, unable to distinguish any longer between the promptings of real or feigned moral principle.

And for a considerable time he succeeds in doing just that. When he is once in the Cabinet and up to his neck in the blood of fallen officeholders, he can convince Mrs. Lee that, though he is unable to stop the carnage, he must remain in office "to prevent what evil he could, not to be responsible for the evil that was done." She is thus brought to a baffled submission before the apparent necessity of apparent duplicity: "She reconciled herself to the Ratcliffian morals, for she could see no choice. She herself had approved every step she had seen him take. She could not deny that there must be something wrong in a double standard of morality, but where was it? Mr. Ratcliffe seemed to her to be doing good work with as pure means as he had at hand. He ought to be encouraged, not reviled. What was she that she should stand in judgment?"

Simultaneous with the blunting of Mrs. Lee's moral sense is Ratcliffe's attempt to direct her wish for self-sacrifice to himself. In this he shows perhaps an even more fiendish cunning, for he discovers precisely where she is most vulnerable, and is willing, without a second thought, to turn her innocent weakness to his own advantage. In building himself up as superior to his surroundings, as a steady though not quite self-sustaining beacon in the darkness, he appeals almost irresistibly to her "woman's natural tendency towards asceticism, self-extinction, self-abnegation."

> What woman with a soul could see before her the most powerful man of her time, appealing—with a face furrowed by anxieties, and voice vibrating with only half-suppressed affection—to her for counsel and sympathy, without yielding some response? . . . Surely a man who spoke as he spoke had noble instincts and lofty aims? Was not his career a thousand times more important than hers? If he, in his isolation and his cares, needed her assistance, had she an excuse for refusing it? What was there in her aimless and useless life which made it so precious that she could not afford to fling it into the gutter, if need be, on the bare chance of enriching some fuller existence?

Here, then, are the elements of *Democracy*'s fundamental moral predicament: in Mrs. Lee, the search for a meaning in life, combined with ambition sublimated by the will to self-sacrifice; in Senator Ratcliffe, pure egoistic craving for mastery, armed with the temptation of power which is masked as the opportunity for virtuous action. Even if his dramatization is not fully equal to its possibilities, Adams' creation of this predicament is a serious and brilliantly thought out piece of work.

Its climax and disentanglement come, as with the political theme of the book, in the long scene during which Mrs. Lee confronts Ratcliffe with Carrington's letter and refuses his proposal of marriage. Her reasons for this refusal, both implied and stated, constitute the central moral position of the novel. There are three of them. The first is that Mrs. Lee finally recognizes, in the naked light of Carrington's revelation, the extent to which she has been seduced by her own ambition. Her disappointment is greater with herself than with Ratcliffe. In "the depths of her soul" she suddenly reads "ambition, thirst for power, restless eagerness to meddle in what did not concern her, blind longing to escape from the torture of watching other women with full lives and satisfied instincts, while her own life was hungry and sad. . . . The worst . . . disappointment [was] in the discovery of her own weakness and self-deception." Since we realize, however, that Mrs. Lee's ambition was not simply thirst for power and that her "tendency towards asceticism, self-extinction, self-abnegation" was not simply a deception, there is more implied by this severe judgment of Mrs. Lee upon herself than meets the eye. The judgment suggests an absolute condemnation by Adams of the desire for power, even if the desire is weak and even if it is qualified by the best intentions. *Democracy* signals a revulsion on Adams' part from all contact with power; the book distinctly reflects his wish to extirpate in himself any lingering traces of the old hankering after a political career, a hankering that was perhaps his chief motive in life during much of his youth. One of the things Mrs. Lee's rejection of Senator Ratcliffe says is that power corrupts, even the mere wanting of it.

The second reason for Mrs. Lee's refusal to marry the Senator is connected with her reasons, mentioned above, for being disenchanted with democracy. The basic structure of *Democracy* as a novel is that of a quest by Mrs. Lee, on one level for the secret of democratic government, on another for a meaning of life. These are, in effect, the same thing, since she is prepared to find in democracy a possible meaning for her life. When, therefore, she comes to the conclusion that democracy is "like any other government" and that it consists in meaningless egotism devoid of political significance or any impersonal value, her quest in both of its aspects is clearly designated a failure.

So far as democracy is concerned this failure is not hard to understand; but what does it mean to say that Mrs. Lee has failed to discover a meaning for her life? What is such a meaning? The answers to these questions are implicit in the very terms of Mrs. Lee's quest and her failure; they are the grounds upon which her repudiation of Ratcliffian democracy is based. The moral color blindness, the egotism, of Senator Ratcliffe and the government he stands for are what they are precisely because democracy has no final, impersonal goal transcending the mere exercise of power. Without such a goal power inevitably leads to the corruption so bitterly and gleefully pointed to by Baron Jacobi. Without such a goal—an "object worth a sacrifice"—government inevitably falls victim to partisanship with its spurious loyalties and sacrifices of principle. Mrs. Lee embarks upon her quest for democracy's meaning with the expectation, or at least the hope, of finding what Adams knows democracy has already lost and only possessed during the brief ascendancy of Jeffersonian Republicanism. Then, a man like Gallatin could see history as a progress toward an ideal and his own life as deriving its value from service to the cause of progress. The ideal was, *par excellence,* an "object worth a sacrifice." But contemporary democracy, in Mrs. Lee's and Henry Adams' eyes, is void of ideals, hence incapable of providing a meaning for life to one in whom meaning is identified with "asceticism, self-extinction, self-abnegation." The meaning of life must exist elsewhere than in the ego.

Thus, the action and moral judgment of *Democracy* are dependent upon one principle which is more important to Henry Adams' mind than any other that can be elicited from his books. For him, value or meaning is only conceivable as originating in final, impersonal ends. He cannot think of life as having meaning apart from a goal that is outside of and larger than the individual. This is the most fundamental and omnipresent manifestation of his Puritanism; it is a mental habit shaped by the obsessive need of his conscience to relate every event, every moral act, and every individual self to some ultimate and all-embracing unity. In the words of Yvor Winters, "There is no knowledge, for Adams, [and hence no meaning] unless it is a part of a complete system, deriving from an acceptable definition of the Absolute. . . ." [2] The Absolute might be a political ideal, an historical order, or a cosmology; whatever its nature at various moments of his intellectual career, its presence or absence determined the intelligibility of life for him. To people like Mrs. Lee or Henry Adams, when the Absolute was lost or proved illusory, life became an agonized absurdity. Without the transcendent, impersonal ends in which the Absolute was embodied, the individual was doomed to a blind and isolated pursuit of self-gratification. Without such ends, society was a pointless Hobbesian war of every man against every man, or interest against in-

2 *In Defense of Reason* (New York: Swallow Press and William Morrow, 1947), p. 399.

terest, or party against party. Mrs. Lee's quest is for some end beyond herself, in the goodness of which she can reasonably believe, and the attainment of which she can make the purpose of her life's effort. As she is conceived by Adams, there can be no other source of meaning for her besides such an end, and if she fails to find it in democracy, then she must simply do without. At the close of the novel, her life is just as meaningless to Mrs. Lee as it was at the beginning. It is, in fact, "emptier than ever now that his dream [is] over."

The third reason for Mrs. Lee's rejection of Senator Ratcliffe is closely connected with the foregoing one and it reveals almost as much about the way Henry Adams' mind worked. Once Mrs. Lee has found out the disillusioning truth of democracy, and felt palpably the corruption that has begun to cling to her through her association with Ratcliffe, her only thought is to extricate and "protect herself," to "quit the masquerade." "I will not share the profits of vice," she says, "I am not willing to be made a receiver of stolen goods, or to be put in a position where I am perpetually obliged to maintain that immorality is a virtue!" Whether or not her life has found a meaning, she must preserve her integrity; she must be able to tell herself that stolen goods are stolen goods and that immorality is not a virtue but immorality. If she knows anything at all, it is that her moral senses must not be allowed to atrophy as have Ratcliffe's. We need not trouble ourselves about the content of these "moral senses." Obviously Adams has nothing else in mind than the most commonly accepted moral assumptions of our society. But Mrs. Lee appeals not to their common acceptance, or to their eternal rightness, or to their divine sanction, but to the simple fact that she believes in them and that to deny her belief would be an unthinkable violation of herself. In opposition to Ratcliffe's moral blindness she upholds the value of integrity, the one sure sanction that she has for keeping aloof from the double standards of modern politics. Integrity, and nothing else, requires that she not tell lies to herself, that she not enter the twilight world where corruption is the best means available for a noble end and ambition is called devoted service of "this glorious Union, the last hope of suffering humanity."

In proof of the value her integrity has for her, Mrs. Lee ends the book with the most dramatic gesture Adams could imagine (within the bounds of propriety)—she flees. To so rescue oneself, Adams thinks, is the best one can do, faced with the intractable, contagious evil of the world of politics. But at the same time, we are well aware that to escape is to give up the hope for meaning and purpose and to accept a life now "emptier than ever." With an empty life, albeit her self-respect is still intact, and with a kind of free-floating moral consciousness unattached as yet to any final goal, Mrs. Lee departs for Europe and the Nile on what may, for all we know, be the first of a series of voyages. The image might have haunted Adams like a prophecy.

4

ᐱᔧ JOHN RANDOLPH

ALL OF Henry Adams' early works, except the *History,* have been
largely ignored by readers and critics alike, but *John Randolph*
has more nearly fallen into oblivion than any of the others. If this
indicates that a low opinion of the book is commonly held, even among
close readers of Adams, then a great injustice has been done to a minor
masterpiece of critical biography. Adams himself, no doubt, has contributed much toward giving such an opinion currency, but his public
attitude toward his own books was always one of ironic depreca-
tion, and in the case of *Randolph* his scorn for its subject made him
talk as though the book deserved just as much contempt as the man—
"Don't read him," he warned John Hay of *Randolph,* "should you by
chance meet him. Kick him gently, and let him go." In another letter
he spoke of his boredom with "correcting the proofs of a very dull
book about John Randolph, the fault of which is in the enforced obligation to take that lunatic monkey *au sérieux.*" Remarks like these
seem to have convinced his readers that Adams' biography of Randolph was not to be taken *au sérieux,* even though he would never
have permitted himself to publish—in the American Statesmen series,
at that— a careless or undignified piece of work.

The writing of *John Randolph* illustrates the kind of energy, itself a
form of genius, Adams had at his command during the years between
his return to Washington in 1877 and the death of his wife in 1885.
When he was invited to contribute to the American Statesmen series
by its general editor, John T. Morse, in late March or early April,
1881, Adams was hard at work on his *History.* He wrote his acceptance
to Morse on April 9th; exactly three months later he announced the
book "finished," and on the same day told Gaskell that he had completed the first two volumes of the *History.* (Both manuscripts were
of course first drafts. *John Randolph* was not published until October,
1882). The speed with which *Randolph* was composed had a most
fortunate effect on this occasion for it resulted in an exceptional unity
of tone and style and a concentrated brilliance rare in the art of political biography. To be sure, *Randolph* is not, like the *Gallatin,* a full-

scale biography; it is not even exhaustive with respect to politics; nor is it thickly sown with the documents of "scientific" historiography. But in page after page it is luminous with a prose equal to the best of the *History,* which is very good indeed. Its style is for the most part swift, supple, and epigrammatic, perfectly suited for the trenchant condensation and irony required by Adams' intention. It is a beautifully controlled style, capable of summarizing the major issues of political debate without damage to nuances of meaning, capable too of sharply drawn portraiture that nevertheless retains the flavor of complex life.

Randolph's limitation of scope undoubtedly goes far to explain its intensity of effect. As a political biography it concentrates on a relatively small number of events, and it narrowly confines the interpretation of these events within the bounds of a single theme. This theme is once again the failure of Republican idealism, but only as it occurred in the area of constitutional doctrine. In *Gallatin* Adams pointed out the importance of constitutional theory to the Republicans, and Gallatin himself considered it one of the two principal questions with which he was engaged as a congressman. But Gallatin's necessary absorption in economic affairs drew Adams away from this subject and tended to minimize its significance in the rise and fall of the Republican movement. Randolph, on the other hand, was a veritable embodiment of Republican strict constructionism. The principle of states' rights was to him "always an inspired truth which purified and elevated his whole existence; the faith of his youth, it seemed to him to sanctify his age." It had a direct immediacy for him as a Virginian whose allegiance was primarily to his own state. Gallatin, and Jefferson too, in their fear of national authority and defense of state sovereignty, were actually more concerned with a generalized ideal of human freedom drawn from the sources of French and English revolutionary liberalism. Randolph stood for traditional regional independence and the constitutional program in which the uniquely American aspects of eighteenth-century liberalism took their form.

In his study of Randolph's career, then, Adams is almost exclusively occupied with the fate of the doctrine of states' rights. The foundation of this doctrine, as he sees it, was "the historical fact that political power had, in all experience, tended to grow at the expense of human liberty." It did so because every historical government had been able to define its own power over the governed, and naturally sought to increase rather than diminish that power. Somewhere in every government, like a prehistoric sting in its tail that evolution refused to make obsolete, was an ultimate irresponsibility, a final appeal to force by which the will of an individual or a body of men could be imposed upon the governed community. The doctrine of states' rights was designed specifically to remove the sting of government. Its intention was to fix "a barrier against this supreme central power called national sovereignty, which, if left to grow unresisted, would repeat here all the miserable experiences of Europe." Its successful practice enjoined, as the *Life of Gallatin* showed, "the utmost economy, because extravagance generates corruption, and corruption generates despotism"; a weak executive more or less dependent on a stronger legislature; and as clearly defined and charily granted rights of power as possible. "But, above all, the States must be supported in exercising all their reserved rights, because, in the last resort, the States alone could make head against a central sovereign at Washington." Such a system, Adams finds, "implied a policy of peace abroad . . . leaned rather towards a confederation than towards a consolidated union, and placed the good of the human race before the glory of a mere nationality."

This definition is consistent with Adams' attitude toward Republicanism in the *Life of Gallatin*. What gives coherence to Adams' treatment of Republicanism in both these books is his unerring sensitivity to the idealism that motivated it. The states' rights principle, he never fails to remind his readers, originated in a noble impulse, however "hateful" to "a generation like our own" the term may have become "owing to its perversion in the interests of negro slavery." Before being perverted, states' rights were rationally justifiable as a bulwark against "all the miserable experiences of Europe," its despotisms, wars, poverty, and hopelessness of change. The men who struggled to ensure states' rights and to build up a permanent political structure upon them cherished just such a hope of change. Their ultimate good was neither personal nor local but the "good of the human race." By shackling power and making freedom for once secure and inviolable, they foresaw a great liberation of humanity, an irresistible movement toward the perfection that lay within man's capacities. The states' rights principle was, in short, one form of Republican confidence in human nature and progress, one form of the democratic idealism to which the world's best hopes were pinned during the Age of Jefferson.

Randolph gets from Adams all the credit due him for his participation in the lofty spirit of early Republicanism. As a young congressman he was a fervent and high-minded idealist; he *was* "purified and elevated" by his faith, even though his age only *seemed* to be sanctified by it. Adams repeatedly calls attention to his honesty of purpose and his integrity in the first years of his political career, and hesitates before he attributes Randolph's shortcomings to suspicious motives. But suspicious motives undeniably do enter into the picture quite early, and Adams' contempt grows from page to page as he watches the progressive deterioration of Randolph's youthful idealism toward "an overpowering egotism [and] a consuming rage for notoriety." For Randolph was to Adams the prototype of corrupted idealism; this biography is a study in the destruction of idealism by the overmastering force of self-love.

John Randolph, therefore, very much like *Democracy,* has two aspects which are closely related. Its subject is Republicanism which is embodied in a man who is the representative of a particular idea (an idea that is allowed, for the purpose of concentrating dramatic energy, to stand for the whole of Republicanism). In *Democracy* the man and the idea are one; in *John Randolph* such complete identification would have been untrue as well as tortuous, but the life of the man and the life of the idea run intimately parallel to one another, and in doing so they reveal a shift in Adams' attitude towards Republicanism since *Gallatin* and a new focus of interest among the causes of its failure, namely power. The writing of *Democracy* with its critique of politics shows its influence here. For the states' rights idea, which is the vehicle of Republican idealism in *Randolph,* is betrayed not primarily by "circumstances" but by the Republicans themselves, whose idealism is corrupted by the possession of power. Concomitantly, Randolph, the idealist, is corrupted not by an excess of the doctrinaire spirit but by his ambition which, given his political impotence, eventually takes the form of "a consuming rage for notoriety, contemptible even in his own eyes." The moral of *John Randolph* is that power and the love of power corrupt; it is the moral of *Democracy* applied to Republicanism.

In demonstrating this moral, Adams' chief instrument is an ironic method which consists essentially in the juxtaposition of thought and action in such a manner as to emphasize the gap between them. It is a very simple method, but employed deliberately and exhaustively, it permits extremely refined insight into motives. Adams first brings it into play in Chapter III of *John Randolph* which covers the initial two years of Jefferson's presidency. His first step is to show what the intentions of the Republicans were when they came into office in 1801. He quotes from Randolph's letters in which the zeal for reformation of a Federalist-styled government is impatient and uncompromising: "Without a *substantial reform* we shall have little reason to congratulate ourselves on the mere change of *men.*" Adams notes Randolph's suspicion of his fellow party members' adulation of Jefferson which, to Randolph's "true republican" sensibilities, smacked of monarchy. He refused to be the captive of an individual or even of his own party; in fact, "to be jealous of executive influence and patronage was the duty of a true Republican, and to wear the livery of a superior was his abhorrence."

With these convictions fixed in his mind, Randolph knew precisely the direction he wanted his "substantial reform" to take. The "dogmas of [his] creed" were "dread of the Executive, of corruption and patronage, of usurpations by the central government; dread of the Judiciary as an invariable servant to despotism; dread of national sovereignty altogether. . . ." The task of reform was that of "correcting past mistakes" made by the Federalists in violation of all these dogmas, "and of establishing a new line of precedents to fix the character of future politics." The Republicans, as they assumed the national reins, were eager for this task and were remarkably well prepared. Their leaders had ability and popularity; they had received a strong mandate from the people; and they had a program which "during twelve years of opposition" they had "hammered out . . . on the anvil of federalism." Above all, they had a fresh, idealistic drive: "Mr. Jefferson and his Virginian followers thoroughly believed themselves to have founded a new system of polity. Never did any party or any administration in our country begin a career of power with such entire confidence that a new era of civilization and liberty had dawned."

But what was the outcome of these great plans and expectations? Adams finds that although "Randolph's own wishes would have favored a thorough revision of the Constitution and the laws . . . The President and the Cabinet shrank from strong measures." True, the northern democrats were a little weak in their loyalty to the party program, and "the Senate was still narrowly divided," but "the real reason for following a moderate course lay deeper than any mere question of majorities. The republican party in 1801 would not touch the true sources of political danger, the executive and legislative powers, because they themselves now controlled these powers, and they honestly thought that, so long as this was the case, states' rights and private liberties were safe." What a judgment is implied by these words! The key to Adams' whole attitude toward Republicanism in this book is contained in them. Adams transfers Ratcliffe's "double standard of morality"—one for himself and one for his enemies—to the great Republican party, the party of Jefferson and Madison.

Shrinking from strong measures, the Republicans were nevertheless committed to reform, and in the first couple of years the most urgent problem calling for reform, Adams thinks, was the judiciary. They were confident in their control of the executive and the legislature, but the judiciary, which had been created and manned by Federalists, was potentially a "fatal obstacle" to the security of their new system, "for until the fountain of justice should be purified the stream of constitutional law could not run pure, the necessary legal precedents could not be established, the States could not be safe from encroachments, or the President himself from constant insult." The Republicans, therefore, set about cleansing the federal judicial system by passing a bill which abolished the new circuit courts and judgeships created in the last days of John Adams' administration. This bill is given a rather extensive evaluation by Adams as the first important clue to the weakening by power of Republican moral fibre.

The Republicans well knew, he thinks, that what was required for their purposes was a thorough reconstruction of the judiciary in order to make it weaker than the state courts and accessible to legislative control. They knew, furthermore, that the cornerstone of the federal judiciary was the Supreme Court, that "Chief Justice Marshall and the Supreme Court, backed by the array of circuit and district judges, could always overturn republican principles and strict construction faster than Congress and the President could set them." A revolution of the country's legal system was needed to remove this stumbling block. But what did the Republican reform bill, the Repealing Act, accomplish by way of revolution? This act, which abolished the new circuit judgeships created by the last Federalist Congress, "was in fact not revolution, but concession; overthrowing a mere outer line of defense, it left the citadel intact, and gave a tacit pledge that the federalist supreme bench should not be disturbed, at least for the present." The Republicans satisfied themselves by abolishing the circuit courts, but they "let Chief Justice Marshall slip through their fingers," the same Marshall who "in the course of his long judicial career, rooted out Mr. Jefferson's system of polity more effectually than all the Presidents and all the Congresses that ever existed."

What was the cause of Republican weakness and failure at this first critical juncture in their plan to "correct past mistakes . . . and . . . fix the character of future politics"? The broad reason, namely that they "would not touch the true sources of political danger" because they themselves were in power, has been mentioned. But Adams shows this cause working itself out in the behavior of Randolph—of all people!—during the debate over the Repealing Act in the House. Randolph was one of the fiery members of the Virginian school, and probably favored a more radical measure than the bill he defended. But he was restrained by the party high command, and by something else —there was a peculiar lack of zeal against national authority in his arguments, an unwillingness to push his ideas to their logical conclusions. Randolph had the opportunity, according to Adams, of basing the Repealing Act on the solid ground of states' rights principle, "a principle of which any man, who honestly believed in it, must be proud." He might then have treated the Act as merely the first step in a process intended to revolutionize the judiciary, which was its only sound justification, since without such an end in view it had the strange effect of being itself a "blow at the very doctrine of strict construction, since it strained the powers of Congress by a dangerous precedent, without touching the power of the Judiciary." Adams emphasizes this point by a striking shift to the obligatory mood: "Surely this was the moment [when he made his argument for the Repealing Act] for laying down those broad and permanent principles which the national legislature ought in the future to observe in dealing with extensions of the central power; now, if ever, Randolph *should* have risen to the height of that really great argument which alone justifies

his existence or perpetuates his memory as a statesman" (my italics).
But Randolph failed to do what he should have done. The Act "was
the first of many instances in which Mr. Jefferson's administration un-
intentionally enlarged and exaggerated the powers of the general government in one or another of its branches."

The judiciary incident shows very clearly the deflection of Republican idealism by the magnetic attraction of power. Between the
intention and the act falls the shadow of unwillingness to risk the
loss of power, even prospectively, so that the result is an ironic reversal of intention and "the powers of the general government," instead of being diminished, are "enlarged and exaggerated." Randolph's special guilt is underscored by Adams. He remarks that if "the
republicans were over-confident in their own strength and in the permanence of their principles . . . Mr. Jefferson and John Randolph
were responsible for their trouble."

> The party had really fought against the danger of an overgrown gov-
> ernmental machine, but Mr. Jefferson and John Randolph had told
> them they were fighting against monarchy. . . . Randolph saw from
> time to time that, so far as there had been any monarchy in question,
> the only difference was that Thomas Jefferson instead of John Adams
> wore the shadow of a crown, but even Randolph had not the perspicac-
> ity or the courage to face the whole truth, and to strike at the very
> tangible power which stood behind this imaginary throne. He, like all
> the rest, was willing to be silent now that his people were masters; he
> turned away from the self-defined, sovereign authority which was to
> grind his "country," as he called Virginia, into the dust; he had, it may
> be, fixed his eyes somewhat too keenly on that phantom crown, and in
> imagination was wearing it himself,—King John II.

The notes of betrayal and corruption which are struck for the first
time in Chapter III are thereafter repeated insistently by Adams. The
fourth chapter, which is entitled "A Centralizing Statesman," has as
its main subject the Louisiana Purchase, another crisis in the career of
the states' rights principle. Adams shows that the Republicans well
understood their action, however desirable and popular, to be a clear
violation of the Constitution. "From the ground which Mr. Jefferson
and his friends had consistently taken, the Constitution was a carefully considered compact between certain States, with a view to union
for certain defined objects; any measure likely to alter the fixed relations and the established balances of the Constitution without an
amendment required the consent of all the parties. . . ." There was
no doubt that the Louisiana Purchase overthrew the fixed relations and
established balances of the Constitution. It made the federal government sole master of a vast extent of territory bigger than the states
themselves; and it opened up the possibility of the admission of many
new states. It raised a very serious question of constitutional law: who

had the legal right to sanction a purchase like this—the States? Congress? the president? Was it not the moral duty of the government to seek "the consent of all the parties" to the constitutional compact?

Jefferson himself was filled with qualms. Louisiana had been acquired by treaty, but Jefferson was sure he had committed an act, as he said, "beyond the Constitution" and that the government must "throw [itself] on the country for an act of indemnity." He drew up an amendment for legalizing the purchase; urged, even implored, his supporters to back it; but the party, "perverted by the possession of power, would not hear of amending the Constitution or seeking indemnity." Jefferson's friends "persisted in their own contrary opinion, and in the end he acquiesced." The Louisiana Purchase was thus accomplished by the national government's treaty-making power: "It was the perfectly independent act of President Jefferson and twenty-six senators."

Randolph again on this occasion contributed his share to the party's fall from purity. He replied to a Federalist attack on the constitutionality of the purchase with a strange medley of arguments drawn from Federalist precedent and the vagueness of the treaty of 1783, and even resorted to an equivocal interpretation of the terms of the purchase treaty itself. But "He who had raged with the violence of a wild animal against the constitutional theories of Washington and John Adams did not whisper a remonstrance against this new assumption of power, which, according to Mr. Jefferson, made blank paper of the Constitution." The reversal of roles witnessed in the *Life of Gallatin* thus becomes once more an element of the Adamsian irony. The Federalists defend states' rights; the Republicans, in the saddle, ride roughshod over them. "From this moment," Adams observes, "it became folly to deny that the general government was the measure of its own powers, for Randolph's own act had changed theory into fact, and he could no more undo what he had done than he could stop the earth in its revolution."

⋘ ⋙

From this point on there is no reason to chart in further detail the development of Adams' theme and point of view in *John Randolph*. The book continues to trace out the process of degeneration both in party principle and in Randolph himself, until it culminates in the infamous union of states' rights and Negro slavery, a union presided over by the former idealist, John Randolph. Ideologically, perhaps its climax is in Chapter VI, which is almost entirely given over to a study of the impeachment trial of Supreme Court Justice Chase. This trial, says Adams, "is a landmark in American history, because it was here that the Jeffersonian republicans fought their last aggressive battle, and, wavering under the shock of defeat, broke into factions which slowly abandoned the field and forgot their discipline." Their final attempt to control the judiciary defeated, the Republicans gradually lost more and more of their attachment to the doctrine of states' rights; idealism waned, and left in its stead "corrupt factions to dispute with each other the possession of merely selfish power."

As for Randolph, having gone far enough with his party to assist materially in the subversion of those principles "which alone justified his existence," he soon forgot his own discipline and became a faction of one. Full of ambition, and conceiving himself as the lone adherent of "old republican" doctrine among a crowd of timeservers in livery, he began a war on Madison which quickly alienated him from the Republican administration. Adams concedes that there was something grand, if not admirable, in the opposition with which he faced his own leaders. "Mean ambition does not work in such paths; only a classical, over-towering love of rule thus ventures to defy the opinion of others. . . . Office he did not want, and he willingly flung his chances away, but only to grasp at the higher, moral authority of a popular tribune." However, neither his temper nor his patience were controllable; he quarreled with everyone, with Gallatin, with Monroe, to whom he had attached himself in a last effort to revive his prestige, with the closest members of his family. Frustrated and impotent, his mind became unpredictable, his speeches incoherent, and in his relations with fellow congressmen "he carried terrorism . . . to an extreme." The last picture of him that Adams leaves us with is of a man to whom remained "only an overpowering egotism, a consuming rage for notoriety"; he was a jockey "thrown early out of the race, who rides on, with antics and gesticulations, amid the jeers and wonder of the crowd," despising himself but unable to stop, a brutalized and rotten spectacle, "half-insane [and] half-intoxicated."

The chief difference between the *Life of Gallatin* and *John Randolph* is that in the former, democratic idealism fails because it cannot control all the circumstances of life and cannot bend to them without breaking, while in the latter it is "perverted by the possession of power." Adams does not go quite so far as to say that idealism necessarily leads to such perversion, but power does, and idealism, therefore, must fail once it acquires power. The idealistic impulse, in short, is a hopeless one. But this does not excuse corrupted idealists from moral responsibility. Adams holds the Republicans to strict account for the loss, not of perfection, but of their integrity. The whole force of his ironic method is concentrated on this point: they professed idealism; they acted weakly or selfishly; they must be judged ignominious failures. Moral condemnation is perhaps the most lasting impression the book makes. Adams simply could not digest with equanimity the fact of Republican self-betrayal; he returns to it again and again with a kind of fascinated horror.

In a strange way Adams is like a partisan who finds himself deserted by his leaders. Behind his revulsion one senses the instinctive pull democratic idealism exerted upon his sympathies. But, being deserted, he is bitter against his sympathies; he punishes himself and those who have misled him for the humiliation of defeat in which he is implicated but for which he is not responsible. One of the most obvious indexes of his bitterness is his treatment of Jefferson. Whereas in *Gallatin* Jefferson was worthy of being placed side by side with Washington, an essentially noble though occasionally weak man, in *Randolph* he stands not much higher than Randolph himself. He did not, of course, suffer the kind of radical degeneration that Randolph did, but morally speaking, he was no less responsible for the perversion of idealism by power; perhaps he was more so. Holding the position of greatest influence, he might have led the way toward the highest good; instead, without exactly leading, he moved at the head of his party in the direction of failure. He too thought that the power of the executive was safe now that it was in his own possession. "Thus it was that he took into his hand the federalists' constitution, and set himself to the task of stripping away its monarchical excrescences, and restoring its true republican outlines; but its one serious excrescence, the only one which was essentially and dangerously monarchical, he could not, or would not, touch; it was his own office—the executive power."

Everywhere Jefferson lacks the strength to keep his party on the path of virtue. In the Louisiana affair, although "scandalized" by what he had done, he "acquiesced" when the people around him "persisted in their own contrary opinion." In effect, he refused to endanger his prestige and influence by taking a stand against such a popular measure. Caution similar to this was habitual with him. In the impeachment of Justice Chase he was the initiator, the original cause, yet he would not publicly commit himself in such a way as to provide Randolph, who managed the impeachment proceedings, with his support. "Mr. Jefferson was a little too apt to evade open responsibility; the number of instances in which he encouraged others to do what he would not do himself is so large as to strike even careless attention." Adams' attention was not careless, and his notation of these instances suggests the one motive that he thought sufficient to explain them: love of power and the fear of losing it.

From top to bottom Adams saw power corrupting the will of Republican idealism. Senator Ratcliffe, in a subtle act of the mind compounded of fantasy and divination, blends into the image of Thomas Jefferson. Their fusion results in an altered viewpoint which emerges in the *History*, Henry Adams' fullest effort to assess the meaning of America and its democracy.

5

⤳ ESTHER

L IKE *Randolph* and *Democracy*, Henry Adams' second novel, *Esther*, was written quickly and with one hand while he was in the midst of his immense labors on the *History*. It was finished after no more than a few months of work in the fall of 1883, and was published in March of the following year under the pseudonym Frances Snow Compton. Many other details of the publication beside the author's choice of a feminine persona were eccentric. He insisted on an even more rigorous secrecy than that which had surrounded *Democracy*, and refused to permit the publisher, Henry Holt, to advertise it in any way either in its American or English editions. *Esther* was to be an experiment in literary survival, either living or dying by its own merit and the power of word-of-mouth recommendation. Quite predictably, the experiment failed: "So far as I know, not a man, woman or child has ever heard of Esther. . . ."

As in *Democracy*, the characters of *Esther* were based on real people. Clarence King gave many of his features to George Strong, as did John La Farge to the painter Wharton; Phillips Brooks and Elizabeth Cameron provided the models for Stephen Hazard and Catherine Brooke. Most importantly, Adams drew on his wife for the portrait of Esther and this fact led, after her death, to his identification of the novel with her memory and his transformation of it into a kind of tabu-object, simultaneously consecrated and guilt laden. For in December, 1885, Marian Adams committed suicide by swallowing cyanide of potassium, a chemical she made use of in photographic development. The effect on her husband was crushing. He could not bring himself to speak of her for years; all mention of her is omitted from the *Education*. By an enormous act of will he pushed on to the end of his *History*, although he felt the life had gone out of his interest. But *Esther*, he said, had been "written in [his] heart's blood." "I care more for one chapter, or any dozen pages of *Esther* than for the whole history, including maps and indexes; so much more indeed, that I

would not let anyone read the story for fear the reader should pro-
fane it." [1]

Esther, as might be expected, bears certain striking resemblances to
Democracy. Most important of these is in its plot, which again consists in the effort of an intelligent and sensitive woman to ascertain
a meaning for her life. As in *Democracy,* the woman is confronted by
a male embodiment of meaning whose motives of love and domination
are so intertwined as to be inseparable. The novel, therefore, like its
predecessor, culminates in a choice between acceptance and rejection
of the male, a choice on which the issues of personal integrity and
spiritual security depend. Esther's decision to reject her suitor, like
that of Mrs. Lee, saves her freedom and integrity, but at the expense
of cutting her off from an almost achieved purposefulness.

Despite these important similarities, however, it is a mistake to regard *Democracy* and *Esther* as thematically identical, differing only
in subject matter, artistry, and degree of the author's involvement.[2]
The later book goes far beyond the earlier in its exploration of moral
values and its effort to give these values a philosophical justification.
Democracy is, before all else, a political novel; its chief purpose is to
analyze democracy as a system of ends, to get "to the heart of the
great American mystery." Mrs. Lee is the medium through which this
purpose is accomplished; only by implication, and at the end of the
story, are the values upon which she bases her judgment of democracy
introduced into the novel's action.

The case is entirely different with *Esther.* Although Hazard is a
spokesman of orthodox religion and seeks to impose his orthodoxy
upon Esther at the same time that he makes love to her, the novel is
not primarily an examination of religion's claim to impersonal ideality.
Another way of saying this is that the character of Esther is much more
central, the character of Hazard much less so, to the main theme of
the book than are their counterparts in *Democracy.* That theme is the
discovery of moral identity, and the establishment of the value of integrity (which to Mrs. Lee rested on personal, irrational grounds)
upon an impersonal, philosophic principle. Esther alone embodies this
theme entirely, by her falling in love with Hazard, her rejection of
him, and her contemplation, at the book's close, of Niagara.

Here, then, is the essential difference between *Democracy* and
Esther. Mrs. Lee starts out in conscious search of a purpose in life;
after finding out the truth about democracy—which is the point of
the book—she is back precisely where she started. But Esther moves

---

[1] For the similarities between Esther and Mrs. Adams, irrelevant to the present
discussion of the novel, see Ernest Samuels, *Henry Adams: The Middle Years*
(Cambridge: Harvard University Press, 1958), Chapter Seven and pp. 276–80.

[2] For this opinion, see Robert E. Spiller's introduction to *Esther* (New York:
Scholars Facsimiles and Reprints, 1938).

from ignorance to achieved realization of her life's purpose, forced by the logic of events and her own responses to them to a new state of awareness—which is the point of the book. This concentration upon the development of the heroine explains the greater psychological depth of *Esther*, and is the key to its divergence from *Democracy*.

Esther's growth is caused by a pressure similar to that imposed upon Mrs. Lee, yet here too there is a significant difference. Mrs. Lee's motive in permitting Senator Ratcliffe's intimacy is at bottom the wish to sacrifice herself for a worthy and impersonal objective. She is never in love with the Senator, though he acquires a measure of dominance over her. Esther, on the other hand, falls in love with Hazard, which puts his claim upon her in an entirely new light. For Esther's love is the means by which she comes to know her true aim in life; in a very direct sense, Hazard *is* Esther's objective, although he is her nemesis as well. Her rejection of him, therefore, offers a profounder glimpse into Adams' understanding of motivation than Mrs. Lee's dismissal of the Senator.

As in *Democracy*, the decision that the heroine of *Esther* makes with regard to the marriage proposal of the hero is significant in two ways. Mrs. Lee's rejection of Senator Ratcliffe expresses her judgment of contemporary democratic politics, and it implies the choice and affirmation of certain values which are symbolized by her act and its motives. In *Esther* the medium of action is religion, for Hazard is a clergyman who wishes to force the heroine into compliance with his strict orthodox beliefs. Although he is not quite so unsympathetically drawn, Hazard is cut according to the same pattern as Senator Ratcliffe. He is basically an egotist whose religion, however sincerely he may feel it to be true and necessary, is an expression of his will to dominate and possess others. Just as Ratcliffe's love of power is hidden behind his appeal to Mrs. Lee's craving for "asceticism, self-extinction, self-abnegation," so does Hazard's overmastering will come disguised as the love which Esther so much needs and wants.

Hazard's egotism, in fact, is a much more absolute and despotic force than the Senator's. There are two reasons for this. In the first place, Hazard's love for Esther is a good deal less cynical than Ratcliffe's for Mrs. Lee. The latter, we remember, conducts his wooing in accord with "his usual theory of political corruption as applied to feminine weaknesses." When the proper time comes, therefore, Mrs. Lee can see through him and feel duped and betrayed. But Esther is permitted no such advantage in preparing for her dismissal of Hazard. To the very end, she knows that he represents "the romance of her life," and when on the verge of cutting herself off from him forever, she feels her heart "wrung" at throwing away "a love so pure and devoted." Hazard, in other words, does not expose himself, as the Senator does, to a fairly conventional kind of moral revulsion. Esther's decision concerning him is thereby made inevitably more painful, less easily justified while requiring profounder justification, than Mrs. Lee's decision with respect to Senator Ratcliffe.

Secondly, Hazard has, to all appearances at least, a far better claim than the Senator to be considered the representative of a system of ideal ends. It is easy, after all, to believe in the hidden corruption of politics; Adams has only to pin a vote fraud and the acceptance of a bribe on the Senator and we are convinced, along with Mrs. Lee, of his hypocrisy and the hypocrisy of democratic government as a whole. But Hazard is beyond such conventional peccadilloes. He is too passionately earnest in his faith to be susceptible to the kind of temptations that seduce Senator Ratcliffe. The Senator, at bottom, believes in nothing; but when Esther, after listening to Hazard's first sermon, asks her skeptical cousin, George Strong, if Hazard "believes it all," Strong answers, "Yes, he has put his life into the idea. . . . Even at college he would have sent us all off to the stake with a sweet smile, for the love of Christ and the glory of the English Episcopal Church."

Given these advantages over the Senator, in what way, then, does the purer, less vulnerable egotism of Hazard manifest itself? First of all, Adams makes it clear from the start that Hazard's religious mission contains an element of insatiability, a restless compulsion to claim suzerainty over all domains of life, all souls, all thought, all action. "No trace of humility slip[s] into his first sermon" before his new pastorate. On the contrary,

> he took possession of his flock with a general advertisement that he owned every sheep in it, white or black, and to show that there could be no doubt on the matter, he added a general claim to right of property in all mankind and the universe. He did this in the name and on behalf of the church universal, but there was self-assertion in the quiet air with which he pointed out the nature of his title, and then, after sweeping all human thought and will into his strong-box, shut down the lid with a sharp click, and bade his audience kneel.

What is particularly important to the story is that this "right of property" comes in time to include Esther specifically. Hazard's first distinct idea of her is that she represents a challenge to the power of his ministry. He sees in her religious indifference a test of the church's ability to convince, a test, of course, which is simultaneously one of his own power as agent of the church.

> Hazard's instinct told him that his success, to be lasting, depended largely on overcoming the indifference of people like the Dudleys. If he could not draw to himself and his church the men and women who were strong enough to have opinions of their own, it was small triumph to draw a procession of followers from a class who took their opinions, like their jewelry, machine-made. He felt that he must get a hold on

the rebellious age, and that it would not prove rebellious to him. He meant that Miss Dudley should come regularly to church, and on his success in bringing her there, he was half-ready to stake the chances of his mission in life.

Thus Hazard is initially drawn to Esther for a reason quite other than love. This reason, which seems to him an entirely innocent desire to save her soul, remains uppermost in his mind even after he has fallen in love with her. It infuses his love with an intensity that is very attractive to Esther, but at the same time transforms love into a kind of religious mission. Esther is made aware that Hazard's mind is divided between the motives of love and conversion, and that, ultimately, his love depends upon his success in converting her. But to make conditions in love is a form of compulsion, and to introduce ulterior motives is a form of arrogance. In the final analysis, Hazard's love comprises an assault upon the integrity of Esther's character, an assault that demands religious conversion as the sign and proof of surrender.

Esther's defense of herself, like Mrs. Lee's, is the key action of the novel. Her point of departure may be located in a remark of Esther's which Adams treats so casually as to neglect putting it in quotatior marks. "She complained to Wharton," he writes, "of her feminine wa of motive in life." This complaint, made when Esther is about to en her rather dilettantish assistance of Wharton in his decoration of St. John's Church, characterizes Esther prior to her entanglement with Hazard. She is, as Adams apparently could not help thinking of hi. heroines, without aim or object, adrift in life and conscious of an uneasy sense of meaninglessness. She dabbles in art but, as Wharton says, "She is only a second rate amateur and will never be anything more." She dabbles in charity, but "All I do is to tell them [the children a the hospital] stories." She is in a predicament not unlike Mrs. Lee before the latter's arrival in Washington—dissatisfied with herself a her conventional role in society, and longing in secret for some fit casion worthy of laying claim to her untried resources of strength courage and equal to her capacity for passionate commitment.

This occasion presents itself in the person of Hazard with who Esther falls in love after the death of her father. Through his awak ing of her love, Hazard brings to Esther the conscious certainty purpose that Mrs. Lee fails to attain in her Washington experim' Esther finds in love itself the perfect solution to "her feminine w of motive in life." Love to her is an opportunity to give herself to an object outside and more valuable than her own life. She responds to it with a joyous release of feelings very much like Mrs. Lee's "asceticism, self-extinction, self-abnegation." In the first flush of her discovery of love, for example, she takes pleasure in minimizing the obstacle o' Hazard's calling which only shortly before would have seemed to h insuperable. "For the moment she thought that his profession w nothing to her; she could believe whatever he believed and do whatever he did; and if her love, backed by her will, were not strong enough to make his life her own, she cared little what became of her, and could look with indifference on life itself. So far as she was concerned she thought herself ready to worship Woden or Thor, if he did." Love further implies the satisfaction of those primordial feminine needs for home and family through which a woman realizes her inmost nature and fulfills her destiny. In *Democracy* Adams has Mrs. Lee belatedly recognize the inescapable centrality of love and marriage for a woman when she admits that her attempt to find meaning without husband or children, "outside the household," was following a "will-of-the-wisp." Esther verifies this truth far more poignantly than Mrs. Lee in her own experience of love, and in the bitterness of her loss of Hazard.

It is evident that the primary value of love for Esther, and for Adams as well, is its selflessness. But in its nature love is also private, that privacy being the necessary condition of mutual devotion and mutual acceptance between two people. Once she is in love, Esther wants not only to put aside "the vanities of human society," but to re-create her world, so to speak, on the foundation of lovers' intimacy. "She wanted only to be loved and to love, without being thought of, or noticed; to nestle in her own corner, and let the world go by." In this requirement, however, lies the seed of her first irritation and ultimately her complete disenchantment with Hazard, for he is so constituted as to be unable simply to love and be loved and let the world go by. He cannot, that is, exclude from the intimacy of lovers his claim to a right of property in all mankind. The church, which is Hazard's mode of "self-assertion," obliterates for him the distinction between public and private life, just as it obliterates the distinction, essential to love, between his own and Esther's separate, inviolable soul.

Esther first becomes aware of the threat to her love posed by the church when she listens to Hazard's sermon only a day after his declaration to her. Suddenly he seems "far off and strange. He belonged not to her but to the world; a thousand people had rights of property in him, soul and body, and called their claim religion." When he concludes his sermon with an intensely felt "invocation of infinite love," Esther reacts with shock to the suspicion that he has made use of their private relation in order to move and instruct his hearers. She fears almost that his next word will "reveal her to the world. This sort of publicity was new to her, and threw her back on herself until religion was forgotten in the alarm. She became more jealous than ever. What business had these strangers with her love? Why should she share it with them?"

Thus Esther almost immediately finds the church standing between herself and her love. She is "jealous" of it because she senses that

Hazard's commitment to it goes deeper than his love for her and that, finally, his love must depend on his turning her, as her cousin, George Strong, puts it, into "a candlestick of the church." Her subordination to the church in Hazard's mind is the only reason she can see for his almost pitiless exposure of the feelings sprung from their newly established intimacy. Upon returning home, after listening to him, she bursts out to Catherine Brooke, "What am I to do? I don't like church." And her consciousness of this hostility: toward Hazard's role as a clergyman, toward the role she must assume as his wife, toward the secondary place she holds in his affections—all this forces her to recognize clearly that falling in love with Hazard has involved her in an extremely perilous situation. "He believes in his church more than he does in me. If I can't believe in it, he will have to give me up."

Esther now sets about trying to convert herself as a means of saving her love, and the most poignant section of either of Adams' novels traces her desperate effort to overcome, by force of will, the resistance of her own indestructible nature. Adams' characterization of her, however, has prepared us from the beginning for the failure of this effort. One of the chief purposes of the discussion of art in the first half of the novel is to show Esther's lack of sympathy with Hazard's orthodox taste, her blithe unresponsiveness to the traditional symbols of religion. His newly decorated church, with its prophets and saints, strikes her at first as coming "just a little near being an opera-house." (Hazard himself on this occasion reminds her of "Meyerbeer's Prophet.") This impression never leaves her, for later when she has become Wharton's assistant, she remarks, "It [St. John's] has a terribly grotesque air of theater," to which Wharton significantly replies, "It *is* a theater. . . . This is what ails our religion." All of Esther's struggles with the figure of St. Cecilia she has undertaken to paint stem, too, from her inability to adapt her artistic inclinations to the demands of religious propriety. Hazard's idea of decorum in church embellishment is medieval; he lectures Wharton and Esther on "early Christian art" and does his best to force this influence on their work. But despite his assiduity and powers of argument,

> Esther was not a good subject for instruction of this sort. She cared little for what the early Christians believed, either in religion or art, and she remembered nothing at all of his deep instruction on the inferences to be drawn from the contents of crypts and catacombs. . . . She could not reconcile herself to draw the attenuated figures and haggard forms of the early martyrs merely because they suited the style of church decoration; and she could see no striking harmony of relation between these ill-looking beings and the Fifth Avenue audience to whom they were supposed to have some moral or sentimental meaning.

Both Esther's character, insofar as it represents a spirit alien to Hazard's ideals, and her attitude toward church art are perhaps best summarized by Wharton early in the book, in a speech which directly reflects Adams' own view of these matters. After describing Esther as "one of the most marked American types I ever saw," he tells Hazard that she does not belong to his world: "There is nothing medieval about her. If she belongs to any besides the present, it is to the next world which artists want to see, when paganism will come again and we can give a divinity to every waterfall. I tell you, Hazard, I am sick at heart about our church work; it is a failure. . . . The thing does not belong to our time or feelings."

Thus there is, underlying Esther's hostility to the church for its interference with her love, an original and ineradicable difference between her and Hazard. "There is nothing medieval about her"; she is wholly of her place and time, a "marked American type" of the late nineteenth century, whereas Hazard is all medieval in his devotion to tradition and orthodoxy, his confident assertion of the unity of being, and his wholesale confiscation of "all human thought and will" for the service and benefit of the church. To become part of Hazard's world, as Esther wishes to do for the sake of her love, requires her to attempt a radical transformation of her character and sense of the world. What is more, the very meaning of her life, which falling in love has disclosed to her, must be sacrificed to a new meaning that relegates love to a secondary and even utilitarian role.

Faced with such obstacles, Esther's project of self-conversion must necessarily be a wracking experience. The moment of confidence when she thinks she can teach herself to worship Woden or Thor if need be does not last long. For one thing, she finds it simply impossible to resign herself passively to Hazard's spiritual guidance. Her native independence of mind, which had been one of the qualities that had initially drawn him to her, will not let Esther be content with mere acquiescence to Hazard's will. "She could no more allow him to come into her life and take charge of her thoughts than to go down into her kitchen and take charge of her cook." He urges her to avoid the struggle, to leave her doubts and misgivings in his care, "but the moment he was out of sight she forgot that he was to be the keeper of her conscience, and without a thought of her dependence, she resumed the charge of her own affairs." She turns to books to help her out of her difficulties, and is soon entangled in the theological meshes of apostolic succession, the nature of the Trinity, and the authority of tradition. But conviction cannot be hunted down like a rabbit, particularly in such intricate byways. Esther remains unmoved by her reading, except as her failure leads to despair. To George Strong she cries out, "I can't wait. If it [faith] does not come quickly, I must do something desperate." And a few moments later, in response to his pronouncement that she must "Submit!" rather than try to reason herself into faith, she presses her little crucifix against her breast with so much hopeless force that Strong takes it away in alarm at the surge of emotion his words have called forth.

The upshot is that Esther cannot will her own conversion. The materials are not present for it; no life-need of hers is answered by religion, no deep hunger fulfilled by it. Her whole being, in fact, rebels against it as a lie and self-betrayal. Her attempt and failure make her conscious of this as a fixed truth, and henceforth she realizes that she must give up Hazard both to forestall his inevitable renunciation of her and to save her own soul.

Up to this point of decision Esther's reasons for resisting Hazard and all that he represents are, so to speak, purely internal. Like Mrs. Lee, she reacts more or less instinctively against the threat of violation to her personal integrity. But Adams does not let the matter rest here, as he did in *Democracy*. He perceives that to do so in this instance would be both psychologically and rationally insufficient, for Esther is in love with Hazard and must have better grounds for rejecting him than a mere intuitively felt differentness. Therefore Adams conducts his heroine through an experience which completes her self-knowledge, and which fortifies her against her own and the reader's doubt and against Hazard's last appeal to her love.

This experience occurs at Niagara where Esther flees both to escape Hazard and to assert the finality of her decision to refuse him. It is an experience of insight into reality, a confronting of eternal truth through the medium of the immense natural symbol of Niagara. Adams conveys the meaning of this insight obliquely and rather vaguely by means of Esther's conversations with Strong and Hazard and some of her scattered reflections about the waterfall. What follows, therefore, is a somewhat unnaturally systematic version of her final beliefs as they take shape under the influence of Niagara.

The cataract symbolizes to Esther the vast and steady flow of an ultimate energy, of life itself, that satisfies its transcendent purpose through the fullest possible realization of itself within its individual particles. Life is its own end so far as the individual is concerned, but each life has its unique truth, or principle of integrity, which it contributes to the total and eternal meaning of life as a whole. There is no single abstract faith by which eternity is circumscribed; eternity is the mysterious wholeness of life comprising the innumerable particularities of living truth. This, or something like it, is the gist of Esther's metaphor for Strong's conception of a nonpersonal, "scientific" immortality: "Does your idea mean that the next world is a sort of great reservoir of truth, and that what is true in us just pours into it like raindrops?" Her image is drawn from the Niagara waterfall "rambl[ing] on" in the background "with its story, in the same steady voice, never shrill or angry, never silent or degraded by a sign of human failing. . . ." "After all," Esther bursts out after hitting upon her picture of the next world, "I wonder whether that may not be what Niagara has been telling me!"

This is Esther's view of reality, of transcendent good (or at least necessity), which is the source of her individual meaningfulness. The obligation it lays upon her is fidelity to the truth of her own nature, and in the name of that obligation she makes her final stand against Hazard on broader grounds than had heretofore been rationally conceivable to her. Under the influence of Niagara it is the church itself, beyond the cover it provides for Hazard's ego, that Esther rejects. Almost at once, to her mind, the waterfall stands in opposition to the church; the "voice of the waters," she guesses, tells her "a different secret from any that Hazard could ever hear. 'He will think it is the church talking!'" The secret is one precisely the least expected by Hazard in his last interview with Esther. "It must be that we are in a new world now, for I can see nothing spiritual about the church. It is all personal and selfish." Illumined by the message of Niagara, the intuitive hostility felt by Esther throughout the book toward religious orthodoxy is crystallized into a formulable perception of its inadequacy. "I despise and loathe myself, and yet you thrust self at me from every corner of the church as though I loved and admired it. All religion does nothing but pursue me with self even into the next world." The climax of this insight comes in Esther's reply to Hazard's last, nearly incredulous question:

> "Can you . . . think of a future existence where you will not meet once more father or mother, husband or children? surely the natural instincts of your sex must save you from such a creed!"
>
> "Ah," cried Esther, almost fiercely . . . "why must the church always appeal to my weakness and never to my strength! I ask for spiritual life and you send me back to my flesh and blood as though I were a tigress you were sending back to her cubs. What is the use of appealing to my sex? the atheists at least show me respect enough not to do that!"

Esther insists, as Adams has heretofore invariably done, that ends must lie beyond the self, sanctioned by what is impersonally real and true. Such ends alone provide the motives for the "spiritual life" which is Esther's primary need, as it is of all Adams' heroes and heroines from Gallatin on.

❧ ☙

Esther's pointed reference to her femininity in the above quotation brings up the question of the degree to which the novel's meaning is exclusively feminine in application. There is no doubt that Adams regarded women as especially victimized by the conditions of modern life: this is attested by many of his letters, his lecture on the "Primitive Rights of Women," and the *Education*. At the same time, lack of meaningful purpose obviously encompassed everybody; the predicament of Esther and Mrs. Lee is one common to their world, and the *Education* shows in no uncertain terms the agony of mind it induced in Henry Adams. For this reason I believe *Esther*'s scope is wider than, in Professor Spiller's words, "an examination of the moral force resident in the feminine soul." [3] The reality discovered by Esther behind the symbol of Niagara is something to which sex is irrelevant, something which promises the ultimate annihilation of sexual distinctions. It is a reality—or perhaps one should say a divinity—upon which the spiritual life is founded, and this is something different from, though inclusive of, temporal life with its divisions. In short, Adams again, as he did with Mrs. Lee, projects his idea of self into the character of his heroine and asserts his own philosophic convictions through her gradual apprehension of them.

Esther fits coherently into the logic of Adams' development. The effect of his previous work was to undermine democracy as an end, to remove democratic politics from consideration as a field of action because it was no longer a struggle to realize ideals. Yet the compulsion to see life's meaning in absolute terms did not leave him; rather it inspired a lifelong effort to reconstruct a purposive scheme, if not for himself then for history of which he was a part. *Esther* is Adams' first attempt to employ "science" in this effort. During the 1880's he came more and more to think of science as the only method able to cope with the realities of history. This was because, like many nineteenth-century writers, Adams conceived of science as implying the existence of a meta-empirical reality composed of certain irreducible elements and forces that experimental research might distinguish, codify, and eventually synthesize in a framework of natural law. Science was supposed to go below the surface, to identify once and for all the stream by which, as Adams said, men like Jefferson, Madison, and Monroe were carried along "like mere grasshoppers kicking and gesticulating." Hence the scientism of *Esther* results in a kind of vitalism in which life is conceived as an eternal flow of energy manifesting itself in particular creatures and building up thereby the transcendent harmony of its own truth. Individual integrity is thus justified by the higher end to which it contributes, and the sense of right and wrong finds a ground, at least in Esther's case, for its choices and decisions.

[3] *Esther,* p. vii.

6

◄§ HISTORY OF THE UNITED STATES

Henry Adams' *History of the United States of America during the Administrations of Thomas Jefferson and James Madison* is the last fruit of his absorption in the era of American Republicanism. By virtue of its breadth and fullness of detail, its insight and superb narrative art, it ranks among the greatest of historical works in English. In every way it brings to completion the various themes of Adams' earlier writing, and adds a cool, objective detachment that gives the *History* the solidity of a monument. Whereas in the *Life of Gallatin* Adams had been drawn into what was for him a warm partisanship by the tragic heroism of Gallatin's defeat, and in *John Randolph* had been repelled by the spectacle of corrupted idealism, in the *History* he regards the current of men and events from an elevated distance, his sympathies under careful restraint and his eye probing always for the threads that hold the story together and make it meaningful as "a necessary sequence of human movement."

Nevertheless, despite such detachment and restraint, Adams succeeds in evoking an emotional response to the *History* more enduring than that aroused by any or all of his previous books. The reason is that in the *History* he broadens the drama of democratic idealism to make it inclusive of the whole American people. For the first time in Adams' work the horizon extends beyond the limited field of party theory and practice. Republicanism is now interpreted as a national ethos rather than a more or less accidental and localized phenomenon; the Republicans themselves become symbolic of the national character and of the forces latent in national society. To be sure, the *History* is still chiefly occupied with political events, but these events are significant not merely to a handful of political leaders but to the people who have brought themselves to expression in these leaders. Democratic idealism has expanded in Adams' mind to something more than the attitudes and programs of men who are visibly idealists. It is the longing for social perfection of the whole American people; it is a common aspiration that happens to find its expression in Republicanism and happens to run through its historical career in the form of Republican politics. The *History* thus assumes a structural pattern similar to those of Adams' earlier biographies. In this case, however, it is America that sets out under Republican leadership to realize transcendent goals, to make a perfect society. The magnitude of such an effort, and the necessity of recording its failure, involve Adams in a more searching investigation of American democracy and of history than he had ever before attempted.

I

The goal that gives shape and meaning to the whole great sweep of the *History* is announced in Chapter VI of the first volume: "American Ideals." In that chapter Adams sets forth the transcendent object of the American nation, the inchoate vision of a perfect human society which he thinks underlay the rise of Republicanism and its triumph in 1800. The same ideality which he consistently attributed to the Republican leaders he now recognizes to be the manifestation of a profound popular impulse. Thus the coherence and dramatic force of the *History* arise out of the purposiveness which Adams sees at work under the surface presented by the mass of historical facts. By the chapter on "American Ideals" the *History* is pushed off in the direction of a quest already familiar in Adams' works, a quest for absolute ends.

The first requisite, therefore, to an understanding of the *History* is an interpretation of the chapter on "American Ideals." As a piece of historiographic artistry this chapter is remarkable. It is about twenty pages long—the usual chapter length—and entirely free of abstract generalization on the subject which its title announces. Instead, Adams accomplishes a poetic seizure of meaning in his fusion and direct presentation of concrete and abstract elements. For his purpose nothing could have been more daring or more successful. He is dealing, one must remember, not with a formulated idea but with a "shadowy . . . mental condition" diffused among some millions of unthinking people. Out of paradoxical behavior, out of actions whose motive is obscure, out of coincidentally similar efforts in different parts of the country, out of stray bits of conversation or letters, stray moments of bafflement on the part of foreign travelers, out of all these details he puts together an image of that "mental condition" which is the national idealism, the "elusive . . . spirit of American democracy." Despite, or perhaps because of, this method, nothing is left out that is required for the subsequent narrative. All the action has its common source here. The chapter on "American Ideals" is the key to the entire *History* and the highest peak of Adams' historical prose.

❧ ❧

In its largest sense the American Ideal was, to Adams, something radically new as a popular social force in Western culture: a perfectly free society, resting on no authoritarian or supernatural supports, but on perfected individual human nature realizing itself by unhindered, spontaneous growth. Americans believed that men needed only to be set free from the institutional and intellectual confinements of old Europe in order for their latent energies to burst forth in massive social progress. The confidence in human nature, which Adams previously attributed to the Republican leaders, now appears to be a national faith. All the old organizations, thought by Europeans and die-hard New Englanders to be necessary for the conservation of society, were felt to be antagonistic to progress, repressive of the natural capacities for development possessed by every individual. This was why "respectable Europeans," whose reflections on America Adams uses as a counterpoint in his own depiction of the democratic mind, felt "an uneasy sense of remoteness" in the presence of the American democrat—"from Jefferson and Gallatin down to the poorest squatter"—who "believed himself to be working for the overthrow of tyranny, aristocracy, hereditary privilege, and priesthood, wherever they existed." The American feeling was that "artificial barriers," which had in all history kept the range of human possibility within a depressingly narrow compass, must be swept aside for the sake of man's *natural* powers and merits. Americans thought "that the next necessity of human progress was to lift the average man upon an intellectual and social level with the most favored," and in order to establish "this doubtful and even improbable principle" they must throw overboard "the institutions of church, aristocracy, family, army, and political intervention, which long experience had shown to be needed for the safety of society."

In pointing out how thoroughgoing was the American faith in human perfectibility, Adams notes that "this doubtful and even improbable principle"—his words are extremely significant—was entertained in its most doubtful and improbable form by Jefferson, whose opinions "in one form or another, were shared by a majority of the American people." Adams composes a little speech for Jefferson in which "he might be imagined to define democratic progress, in the somewhat affected precision of his French philosophy:

'Progress is either physical or intellectual. If we can bring it about that men are on the average an inch taller in the next generation than in this; if they are an inch larger round the chest; if their brain is an ounce or two heavier, and their life a year or two longer,—that is progress. . . . I expect it to be made here, under our democratic stimulants, on a great scale, until every man is potentially an athlete in body and an Aristotle in mind.' "

But one element is omitted from this definition, and Adams leaves it to "the New Englander" to protest: "What will you do for moral progress?" This question leads most directly to the "chasm" between old and new, European and American. Adams finds that even Jefferson left barely a clue in his writings to the hope he cherished on this point. Yet, all the more because of this, his occasional suggestions are immensely revealing, as when he wrote "in 1815, at a moment of despondency . . . 'I fear from the experience of the last twenty-five years that morals do not of necessity advance hand in hand with the sciences.'" From such a remark Adams concludes that in 1800 "Jefferson held the faith that men would improve morally with their physical and intellectual growth; but he had no idea of any moral improvement other than that which came by nature." Moral growth was simply the complement of physical and intellectual growth, and the expectation of its natural occurrence shows with utmost clarity the profound radicalism of the American democratic ideal in 1800.

In their groping toward this ideal, Americans assumed certain modes of behavior that resulted in a national character marked by curious paradoxes. The universal opinion of travelers from abroad, says Adams, was that American life was dominated by the pursuit of wealth. "In the foreigner's range of observation, love of money was the most conspicuous and most common trait of American character." Every visitor, from Talleyrand to Tom Moore, complained about American hardheadedness and lack of generosity. Yet with strange inconsistency, Republicans were continually being denounced as visionary dreamers. "Every foreigner and Federalist agreed that he [Jefferson] was a man of illusions, dangerous to society and unbounded in power of evil; but if this view of his character was right, the same visionary qualities seemed also to be a national trait." For Jefferson was only the articulate voice of "an emotion which caused the poorest peasant in Europe to see what was invisible to poet and philosopher,—the dim outline of a mountain-summit across the ocean, rising high above the mist and mud of American democracy."

In the ideal itself Adams sees an explanation of the peculiarly American mixture of rapacity and vision. The marshaling of their energies for the next great step of human progress, namely "to lift the average man upon an intellectual and social level with the most favored," was to Americans, in a very immediate sense, a "question of economy." The greatest spur of progress, they felt sure, was after all economic; the dim outline of a mountain summit across the ocean represented to the European peasant, before all else, an opportunity to get ahead in the world, to raise himself by wealth to a higher intellectual and social level. "Wealth was the strongest agent for moving the mass of mankind. . . . The penniless and homeless Scotch or Irish immigrant was caught and consumed by it; for every stroke of the axe and the hoe made him a capitalist, and made gentlemen of his children." Thus the passion for wealth had something more behind it than mere greed. The ideal itself urged men on to transform the untouched continent, rich with possibility, into a paradise commensurate with the impending grandeur of human nature. The visionary quality of American democracy was at one with its pursuit of gain, so that the lonely frontiersman in his wilderness clearing could cry to his foreign visitor:

'Look at my wealth! . . . See these solid mountains of salt and iron, of lead, copper, silver and gold! See these magnificent cities scattered broadcast to the Pacific! See my cornfields rustling and waving in the summer breeze from ocean to ocean, so far that the sun itself is not high enough to mark where the distant mountains bound my golden seas! Look at this continent of mine, fairest of created worlds, as she lies turning up to the sun's never-failing caress her broad and exuberant breasts, overflowing with milk for her hundred million children! See how she glows with youth, health, and love!'

Despite the fact that the European must inevitably respond to such an outburst with " 'Nothing of the sort! I see nothing but tremendous wastes, where sickly men and women are dying of home-sickness or are scalped by savages! Mountain-ranges a thousand miles long . . . swamps and forests choked with their own rotten ruins! . . . Your story is a fraud, and you are a liar and a swindler!' "—despite the prosaic truth of such a reply, Adams thinks the American vision true enough in its own way, at least, to extenuate the charges of greed and ungenerosity. "The hard, practical, money-getting American democrat, who had neither generosity nor honor nor imagination . . . was in truth living in a world of dreams, and acting a drama more instinct with poetry than all the avatars of the East, walking in gardens of emerald and rubies, in ambition already ruling the world and guiding Nature with a kinder and wiser hand than had ever yet been felt in human history."

The "question of economy" was also an important one in determining the American attitude toward restrictive and stratified European forms of society. A large part of the reason why "every American . . . seemed to nourish an idea that he was doing what he could to overthrow the tyranny which the past had fastened on the human mind" was that the kind of economic progress necessary to satisfy his ambition required an absolute freedom of enterprise and a minimum of extraneous expense. The tyranny which the past had fastened on the human mind had stifled progress chiefly through its enormous costliness—the costliness of an aristocracy itself unproductive yet exorbitant in its demands, of Church and State, "holding down activity of thought" and absorbing surplus wealth as fast as it could be made; of wars, debts, and corruption which dissipated every opportunity for progress by mortgaging the future to the vice and extravagance of entrenched powers.

In order to keep themselves free of these heavy financial burdens, Americans were willing to rely on the natural goodness of the individual to preserve social order while giving his natural self-interest free play. "If they could relieve themselves from debts, taxes, armies, and government interference with industry, they must succeed in outstripping Europe in economy of production; and Americans were even then partly aware that if their machine were not so weakened by these economies as to break down in the working, it must of necessity break down every rival." Thus the extreme libertarianism of the American ideal rested on two bases. It depended upon confidence in the natural capacity of human nature to develop morally and intellectually, and it depended upon the necessity for rapid economic expansion. These two motives, Adams thinks, were at the heart of the Republican movement and, more generally, at the heart of the American character at the beginning of the nineteenth century; they give coherence and purposiveness to the acts of the American nation during the Jeffersonian era and they provide a theoretical framework for the policies of that era.

These motives emerged, too, in a distinctive mode of thought which Adams believes was the peculiar manifestation of democratic idealism in practical life. Concretely, the American mind seemed to find its highest natural expression in scientific inventiveness, and Adams points to a list of names including John Fitch, Eli Whitney, and Robert Fulton to prove the activity and variety of achievement in this field. Almost all came from the low or middle strata of society, were therefore typically American in bent and education, and "all their inventions transmuted the democratic instinct into a practical and tangible shape." The democratic instinct took shape in precisely this way because it united science and the economic motive: science, because it is the natural intellectual method of the mind uninhibited (or uninstructed) by church, state, or tradition; and the economic motive, because it represents the desire for progress. The cotton gin, the steamboat, and a dozen other tools symbolize to Adams appropriate strivings of the American mind toward realization of its ideal. "Who that saw only the narrow, practical, money-getting nature of these devices could venture to assert that as they wrought their end and raised the standard of millions, they would not also raise the creative power of those millions to a higher plane?"

Given the foregoing analysis of character and motive, one is led to inquire into the relation between them and the historical narrative that comprises the bulk of the *History*. How did the acts and policies of the Republican administrations flow out of the idealism that gave the Republican movement its impetus? How did these acts and policies represent the impulses of the people? The answers to these ques-

HENRY ADAMS *Bettmann Archive*

tions can be found in the political implications evident in Adams'
statement of American objectives. In the first place, America aimed
at "outstripping Europe in economy of production," a goal whose attainment depended on the ability of Americans to concentrate their
energy and resources in the work of production. Those national re-
quirements which might divert wealth from productive channels had
to be avoided or minimized if at all possible. Thus it was incumbent
upon a government representative of the national idealism that it be
reluctant to impose taxes and equally reluctant to make expenditures.
Such a government must be strictly limited in its functions, both because governmental activity requires money and because it implies the
threat of interference with the private business of individuals. These

specifications describe in general the ideas with which the Republicans
came into office as we have learned to recognize them from Adams'
previous books. The Republican theories of strict economy and strict
construction of federal power under the Constitution conformed to the
essential spirit of American idealism.

The "question of economy" imposed one further requirement of special importance upon the formulators of national policy, namely that
peaceful relations with all countries must be maintained. To Americans war meant the probable reversion of their economy to the normal
European type. "They were tempted to look upon war and prepara-
tions for war as the worst of blunders; for they were sure that every
dollar capitalized in industry was a means of overthrowing their enemies more effectively than a thousand dollars spent on frigates or
standing armies." War inevitably required the shouldering of those
very burdens—"debts, taxes, armies, and government interference with
industry"—whose effects upon the system could well be irreparable.
The cost of war, one might say, was just the difference in wealth
Americans counted on to provide the difference in rapidity of progress
between them and the rest of the world. In the last analysis, the hope
for mental, physical, and moral improvement—the entire superstruc-
ture of American idealism—rested on a fundamental law of policy: the
maintenance of peace. Without comment for the time being, one may
observe that the course of Adams' *History* is actually a long, bitterly
resisted movement toward the climacteric of war.

The "American Ideals" chapter introduces the main theme of the
History and places the eye of the reader at the vantage point from
which the ensuing narrative must be read. Just as in his novels and
biographies Adams interprets the single life by the standards of its
ends and motives, so in his *History* does he interpret the life of a
whole nation. The *History* must be understood as the record of a national attempt to move toward the goals revealed in this key chapter.
The failure of that attempt—for failure it obviously was—is thus the
conclusion to which the whole work tends; the body of the *History*
answers negatively the question posed by the chapter on "American
Ideals": Can these ends be realized? By virtue of its breadth of application and its mass of evidence, this conclusion must be regarded
as Adams' final statement on the subject of democratic idealism.

II

The narrative of the *History* lends itself to a convenient four-part
division. The first of these ends with Chapter X of Volume II and is
chiefly concerned with the internal policies of the new Republican administration. This section is a very careful scrutiny of the actual domestic program of the Republicans, and its relation to the principles
of strict construction and states' rights. The second part, which is

principally occupied with foreign affairs and policy, extends through Volume IV to the end of Jefferson's second term. The Embargo and its failure as a coercive measure conclude this portion of the *History*. In the third section, ending with Chapter XIII of Volume VI, the country is dragged and pushed into war with England as a new spirit of nationality emerges to take the place of the Jeffersonian system. The fourth and last part is almost exclusively about the War of 1812, its military history, the diplomacy that concluded it, and its effects upon the character of the American government and people.

These four parts, once they are discriminated, coalesce into a grand two-part movement of action and reaction. The first four volumes of the *History* show the Republicans' attempt to carry out a revolution by means of new internal and external policies, and they record the failure of the revolutionary enterprise. The last five volumes deal with the consequences of that failure, the readjustment of the national mind to the loss of ideal possibilities, and the reshaping of national policy in accordance with historical actuality rather than a vision of human perfection. In 1800 the goal of the American people, as Adams represents it, was the good of the human race; by 1809 this hope had foundered on the rock of man's permanent limitations; by 1817 America had effectually compromised the ideal by becoming a nation that henceforth must seek its own good, rather than humanity's, in the manner of all other nations. Of course, the tendencies of mind that went into the shaping of the original idealism of 1800 were not extinguished by the succeeding seventeen years. Indeed, Adams finds that they made a lasting impression on the American system. But in the emergence and triumph of an American nationality, these traits, manifested in the familiar doctrines of private enterprise, the balanced budget, isolationism, etc., lost their ideal character and became merely instruments suitable to the working out of America's unique destiny. Thus, although the United States survived and maintained its self-respect, thanks to the awakening of a spirit of nationality, this nationality signified considerably more loss than gain. Nationality is no more than the consequence of decaying idealism; it grows only as faith in the ideal dies; and the displacement of idealism by nationality at the close of the *History* does not mark the welcome beginning of a new era but the end of an ennobling dream. The all-embracing theme of the *History*, therefore, uniting its four minor or two major divisions in a single structure, is the failure and extinction of American democratic idealism, one aspect of which is the rise of American nationality.[1]

---

[1] The conclusion of this paragraph is intended to make clear the divergence of my interpretation of the *History* from that of William H. Jordy who states, "The theme of the *History* is American nationalism." *Henry Adams: Scientific Historian* (New Haven: Yale University Press, 1952), p. 81. The divergence stems, I believe, from different degrees of attention given the works preceding the *History*.

As has already been indicated, the program of Jefferson and his associates, when they took office in 1801, was derived from the vague idealism of a majority of the American people, and represented a concrete means for the achievement of ideal ends. These ends demanded peace, economy, and a government attitude of *laissez faire* except in matters of public law and the dispensation of justice. The Jeffersonian program met these demands exactly. It consisted of three basic policies, all revolutionary in their implications and interlocking so perfectly as to stamp Jefferson's administration with immediate distinction. The first of these was Gallatin's financial policy, which Adams considers to have been the most potent engine of reform actually adopted by the Republican party. Gallatin laid down "the general principle that payment of debt should take precedence of all other expenditure," and the influence of this principle was very soon felt in all the operations of government. It required, in the first place, that most of the federal government's income be put aside out of immediate use, and next that the army and navy, as the chief objects of government expenditure, be reduced to a condition little better than moribund. The Republicans were willing to run the risk of defenselessness for the sake of the purity which Gallatin's scheme imposed upon government. "Freedom from debt and the taxation which debt entailed was his object, not in order to save money, but to prevent corruption." By eliminating the national debt, paring down the armed forces, and keeping the entire governmental organization on a slim budget, all the natural centers of corruption, Gallatin thought, would henceforth be well under control.

Such an economic system had obvious consequences for the powers of government in general. As a matter of fact, it suited quite well the states' rights theory Jefferson brought with him from Virginia. "Gallatin's celebrated financial policy carried into practice the doctrine that the powers of government, being necessarily irresponsible, and therefore hostile to liberty, ought to be exercised only within the narrowest bounds, in order to leave democracy free to develop itself without interference in its true social, intellectual, and economical strength." The theory of states' rights was, from the constitutional point of view, designed for the same ends. Although it was not a uniform creed among the members of Jefferson's party, the doctrine of states' rights was the only coherent legal idea yet thought of that promised what all Republicans were united in desiring: "to leave democracy free to develop itself without interference." States' rights, then, supplemented economy in safeguarding the demand of American idealism for the highest possible degree of personal and economic liberty and the smallest possible amount of institutional restraint.

But one threat to the success of these neatly matched internal policies remained: involvement in war would automatically bring both expense and the centralization of power, a stop to economic progress and an end of perfect liberty. Urgently necessary, therefore, was a foreign policy that could guarantee peace without disturbing the conditions of the domestic experiment. Strength, however, was ruled out as a means of self-protection, at least until the debt had been paid off. Republican economy deliberately emasculated the armed forces, and Jefferson, in any case, disdained strength as a form of barbarism. He believed in the ultimate triumph of rational self-interest in international relations, and he believed that America might lead the way in demonstrating the effectiveness and superiority of a reasonable policy. To preserve American peace he launched his famous substitute for war: "peaceable coercion" by means of commercial restrictions. It was a system remarkable for its strange mixture of naïveté, cynicism, and closefistedness.

> Believing a union of European powers to be impossible, he [Jefferson] was willing to trust their jealousies of each other to secure their good treatment of the United States. Knowing that Congress could by a single act divert a stream of wealth from one European country to another, foreign governments would hardly challenge the use of such a weapon, or long resist their own overpowering interests. The new President found in the Constitutional power "to regulate commerce with foreign nations" the machinery for doing away with navies, armies, and wars.

For Adams, the naïveté of this policy far outweighs its other elements. To face the armed powers of Europe with appeals to their self-interest was to dare "to legislate as though eternal peace were at hand, in a world torn by wars and convulsions and drowned in blood." But Jefferson could not hold back from this attempt; his faith in human nature pushed him on; and he knew, too, that nothing could make his revolution at home more secure or more attractive to the peoples of the world than success in his policy. "Jefferson aspired beyond the ambition of a nationality, and embraced in his view the whole future of man. . . . He would not consent . . . to create more navies and armies, to perpetuate the crimes and follies of Europe; the central government at Washington should not be permitted to indulge in the miserable ambitions that had made the Old World a hell, and frustrated the hopes of humanity." To remain aloof from all contests and to exert pressure only through interest—these were the means by which Jefferson intended to keep his country free of ancient crimes and follies and eventually realize the hopes of humanity.

From this point on, the meaning of the *History* is in the application of Republican policies to national affairs and in the results produced by these policies. Adams dissects the measures in which they were embodied, testing action in the light of intention, weighing and reweighing the force of the revolutionary impulse, continually evaluating success or failure in terms of practicability and progress toward the ideal. In this process of criticism and judgment his earlier ideas about the causes of Republican failure are refined and woven into a sturdier texture than before. There is less tendency to place the blame on one cause and less harshness toward individuals. Failure appears rather more inevitable, not quite so painful as in the *Life of Gallatin,* nor so ignoble as in *John Randolph.* The greater complexity of the *History* leaves less room for moralistic interpretation and draws into view the independent logic of events as well as the sometimes conflicting ambitions of the people and of the Republican leaders themselves. To study these changes, perhaps the best way of reading the *History* is to pay special attention to the concrete differences between it and Adams' previous books.

At the very outset, for example, Adams takes up one of the first Republican actions that exhibited a breakdown of revolutionary principle: the repeal of the Judiciary Act of 1801. In *John Randolph* he chose to regard this step as signifying little else than a moral betrayal of Republicanism by its guardians, carried out in the fear of endangering their power. In the *History,* although Adams still finds Jefferson and his associates guilty on the same score, he is more aware of the attendant political circumstances and not nearly so hasty in making the charge of corruption. Failure of nerve rather than moral obliquity is the dominant impression he conveys, and this is the effect of a more thorough treatment and a greater respect, not for individuals, but for the difficulty of their predicaments.

In essence, the judiciary debate remains for Adams a gauge of Republican earnestness in their program of revolution. The economies carried out by the first Republican-controlled Congress, though radical in intention, could be defended purely in economic terms, but reform of the judiciary demanded a revision of constitutional interpretation that bordered on revision of the Constitution itself. That was why, in the early part of 1802, "The question how to deal with the Judiciary was . . . the only revolutionary issue before the people to be met or abandoned." The Republicans were faced not merely with the Act of 1801 which had created eighteen new circuit judgeships, all filled by Federalists, but with the original Judiciary Act of 1789 which had given the Supreme Court—now headed by the arch-centralizer, Marshall—authority over the state courts in certain matters touching upon the powers of the federal government.

> The effect of both these Acts was, in their [the Republicans'] belief, to weaken the State judiciaries and to elevate the national judiciary at their expense, until the national courts should draw to themselves all litigation of importance, leaving the State courts without character or credit. From their point of view, the whole judiciary system should

be remodelled, with the purpose of reversing this centralizing movement; and that such a reform must begin with the Supreme Court was too evident for discussion. The true question for Congress to consider was not so much the repeal of the Judiciary Act of 1801, as the revision of that which had set in motion the whole centripetal machine in 1789.

In his characteristic manner, Adams thus lays an *obligation* upon the Republicans; he shows them, as well as his readers, the moral duty required of them by their own professions.

The failure of the Republicans to meet and satisfy this call to duty initiates the pattern of failure repeated throughout the entire book. Instead of making a direct and bold attack—as principle entitled them to—upon the source of trouble, the powers of the Supreme Court, the Republicans contented themselves with repealing the Act of 1801, basing the repeal rather ignominiously on the grounds of economy alone. So far as genuine reform went they accomplished nothing. To abolish the circuit courts for economy's sake "would still leave the Judiciary establishment of 1789 untouched, merely in order to lop off an excrescence which might be restored whenever increase of business should require it." Furthermore, by not claiming that abolition of the circuit courts was at least the first step in a thorough reorganization of the judicial system, the Republicans erected, on a ground of pure expediency, a permanent legislative threat against the safety and independence of the judiciary.

What caused this strange misfiring of purpose? In the first place, Adams notes the same reason given in *John Randolph*, the Republicans' overconfidence in their own virtue. Now that they were in power, they felt that states' rights were reasonably safe, despite the danger lurking in the judiciary. Secondly, the Republicans began to have doubts about the political safety of an attack on the Supreme Court; they feared committing an outrage on public opinion and thus losing prematurely the advantages of power. The peculiarities of Jefferson's character were influential in this hesitant policy. "President Jefferson wished to overthrow the Federalists and annihilate the last opposition before attempting radical reforms." But in postponing reform until it could be carried off in perfect safety, Jefferson tipped the balance in favor of the status quo. Adams uses an astute comment by Hamilton to reveal his own opinion of Jefferson's role in the judiciary fiasco. He quotes Hamilton's statement that Jefferson "is as likely as any man I know to temporize, to calculate what will be likely to promote his own reputation and advantage; and the probable result of such a temper is the preservation of systems, though originally opposed, which, being once established, could not be overturned without danger to the person who did it."

One further reason was important in determining the halfheartedness of the Republicans', or at least of Jefferson's, attitude toward judiciary reform. This was the nature of the Constitution itself, which Adams believed had a kind of built-in drive toward centralization, an inherent power to enlarge, by its operation on the holders of office, the scope of federal authority. The Constitution, he thought, worked almost like a natural force in favor of nationalism and against the division of power among the states; even Jefferson and his friends could not resist being drawn into its magnetic field. In the review of Von Holst's *History* mentioned in an earlier chapter, he put this idea more baldly and succinctly than anywhere else:

> It is perfectly true that Jefferson and his party interchanged places with the extreme wing of the Federalists; that each in turn belied its own principles according as each was in power or opposition. . . . The precedents established by the Federalist administrations were accepted and enlarged by the Republican administrations. That Jefferson should have exercised as President powers more questionable than any of those which he had triumphantly assailed his predecessors for wielding, may prove that Jefferson was an unscrupulous politician, but it also proves . . . that the American political system was stronger than the individual, and that the Constitution vindicated its energy in its working.

Thus Jefferson's pledge in his inaugural address to preserve "the general government in its whole constitutional vigor" is noted by Adams as a sign of the immediate influence exerted over him by the Constitution, an influence which, Adams thinks, helped neutralize somewhat his old antipathy to the vigor of the Supreme Court. All in all, what with the added reluctance of northern democrats to follow a bolder Virginian lead, Adams is led to the conclusion that in the Repealing Act "the Virginians had reached not only the limit of their supposed revolutionary projects, but also of their influence, and . . . they were themselves anxious to go no farther."

⊰ ⊱

The analysis of Republican conduct in the matter of judiciary reform is qualitatively different from anything in Adams' earlier books. Not only is it less obviously tendentious and less imbued with emotion, but it bears the subtle impress of a mind in which the consciousness of multiple causality results in what might be called the impersonalization of history. Seeing as much as he does of the complexity in and around events, Adams tends to think of events as forced, as issuing out of their precedent circumstances, more or less beyond the control of individual wills. Not that he is a determinist in the *History;* he is still too much the moralist for that. But the *History* is permeated with a sense of immanent necessity; it dwells harpingly on thwarted intention and the relative unimportance of intention as a cause. The habit of moral judgment requires of Adams that he continue to assign individual responsibility, but he does not believe in that responsibility as he once did. Precisely what he does believe in is not easy to tell. However, from a few casual statements both in and out of the *History* we may derive some clarification of his underlying attitude.

In a letter to Samuel J. Tilden written January 24, 1883, when he was working on Jefferson's second administration, Adams said:

> I am at times almost sorry that I ever undertook to write their [Jefferson, Madison, and Monroe] history, for they appear like mere grasshoppers kicking and gesticulating on the middle of the Mississippi River. There is no possibility of reconciling their theories with their acts, or their extraordinary foreign policy with dignity. They were carried along on a stream which floated them, after a fashion, without much regard to themselves.
>
> This I take to be the result that students of history generally reach in regard to modern times. The element of individuality is the free-will dogma of the science, if it is a science. My own conclusion is that history is simply social development along the lines of weakest resistance, and that in most cases the line of weakest resistance is found as unconsciously by society as by water.

Two years later in December of 1884, when the *History* was "just half done," Adams told another correspondent, Francis Parkman, that

> The more I write, the more confident I feel that before long a new school of history will rise which will leave us antiquated. Democracy is the only subject for history. I am satisfied that the purely mechanical development of the human mind in society must appear in a great democracy so clearly, for want of disturbing elements, that in another generation psychology, physiology, and history will join in proving man to have as fixed and necessary development as that of a tree; and almost as unconscious.

Later, this idea seemed to Adams so important and true as to deserve inclusion in the last chapter of his own great work on democracy.

> Should history ever become a true science, it must expect to establish its laws, not from the complicated story of rival European nationalities, but from the economical evolution of a great democracy. North America was the most favorable field on the globe for the spread of a society so large, uniform, and isolated as to answer the purpose of science.
>
> Travellers in Switzerland who stepped across the Rhine where it flowed from its glacier could follow its course among medieval towns and feudal ruins, until it became a highway for modern industry, and at last arrived at a permanent equilibrium in the ocean. American history followed the same course. With prehistoric glaciers and medieval feudalism the story had little to do; but from the moment it

came within sight of the ocean it acquired interest almost painful. A child could find his way in a river-valley, and a boy could float on the waters of Holland; but science alone could sound the depths of the ocean, measure its currents, foretell its storms, or fix its relations to the system of Nature. In a democratic ocean science could see something ultimate. Man could go no further. The atom might move, but the general equilibrium could not change.

I call these remarks casual because, like all of Adams' pronouncements on the subject of scientific history, they do not cohere very well; to deduce a systematic theory from them would be impossible. The "fixed and necessary development" of a tree, for example, is something altogether different from an ultimate ocean of atoms in equilibrium. Nevertheless, it is not difficult to see that an idea which he had absorbed in London in the 1860's took increasingly strong possession of his mind in the late 1880's. It is an idea of "fixed and necessary" historical change, a process appropriate for scientific analysis like the formation of a crystal or the growth of a tree. For reasons that are not very clear,[2] this process is supposed to be most easily observable in a democracy, particularly that of the United States, and Adams expects such observation to lead to the discovery of the permanent laws that govern the mechanics of change in history.

By this definition the *History* is not scientific. Adams does not deal with the "mechanical development of the human mind in society"; he does not deal with the "economical evolution of a great democracy," nor does he attempt to "measure its currents, foretell its storms, or fix its relation to the system of Nature." In his letter to Parkman he consciously excluded himself from the "new school of history" since it would leave him, as well as his older colleague, "antiquated." His suggestion, in the last chapter of the *History*, that American democracy would be a fit subject for scientific study is an insight passed on to future historians, not an avowal of his own intention. But the idea of necessary movement in history according to some kind of law, whether it be mechanical, evolutionary, or atomic, left its impress on the *History*. It is behind the relatively milder assignments of moral responsibility; it is behind the impersonality of the historical stream, on which men like Jefferson and Madison sometimes seem to float, though they are far from appearing "like mere grasshoppers kicking

---

[2] The reasons Adams gives in the last chapter of the *History* are that America had enjoyed "undisturbed growth"; that being isolated from the "fierce struggle characteristic of European society," it had not become, like the nations of Europe, "chiefly military"; and that its way of life had not favored the emergence of "heroes," who in former times had usurped all the interest of history and of historians. But if laws of history require such conditions in order to be discovered, how applicable are they likely to be to societies that are not undisturbed, isolated, and pacific? Adams' reasoning is very careless. Probably he had in mind the idea that American development had established a pattern toward which Europe must inevitably draw closer, so that America provided a basis for the prediction of *future* changes in the rest of the world.

and gesticulating." A sense of historical necessity also is evidenced in the use of the theme of nationality, an example of which is Jefferson's prompt deference to the vigor of the Supreme Court. The combination of these factors, together with others that have been mentioned, such as complexity of causation, are the whole explanation of what were spoken of before as the *History*'s distinguishing features: monumentality, dispassionateness, and inevitability.[3]

Yet the "free-will" dogma of the science effectually prevented the *History* from becoming a dissertation on the mechanical development of democracies. The true center of the *History*, after all, is not a concern with laws of mechanical development but with the idealism of democracy. The necessitarianism that tinctures the *History* is a response to the failure of idealism; it signifies Adams' conclusion that idealism must have been doomed from the start by the very nature of history. This is why the sense of historical necessity grows more and more evident as Adams' narrative progresses: failure induces resignation to the forces that make failure inevitable. But Adams is never unconscious of the fact that idealism involves its protagonists in a moral struggle as well as in a struggle with the forces of history. In both a logical and a historical sense the moral struggle must, in fact, have priority, since the meaning of the struggle with history depends upon its moral impulse and its effects upon moral outlook. Thus, in the structure of the *History* practical failure is preceded by moral failure; the first great crisis of the book, the Louisiana Purchase, is treated by Adams chiefly as a collapse of Republican morality, setting the stage for the later weakness of Republican idealism in the face of the historical pressures that swept it away.

‹§ §›

The Louisiana Purchase was, for Adams, an event of major importance both to the cause of idealism and to the future character of American government. In itself, and as a precedent, it decisively changed the relation of the federal government to the Constitution as it had previously been understood, and to the states which had contracted their unity under the Constitution. If, as Adams says, in its "Address to the People of the Slave-holding States" of 1860, South Carolina was right in asserting that "The government of the United States is no longer the government of confederated republics, but of a consolidated democracy," then this state must have believed that there had been "some moment in the past when the government must

---

[3] For an excellent discussion of what *was* "scientific" in Adams' approach to the writing of the *History*, see Jordy, *op. cit.*, Chapter I. Jordy summarizes the elements of Adams' scientific attitude as follows: "Emphasis on source materials. An analytic progression. A primary appeal to the reader's intellect. Active reader. Passive historian. The past brought to the reader. The evolution of society, institutions, or a concept larger than its exemplification. Generalizations (seemingly) implicit in the documents."

have changed its character." To Adams' mind, "The only event which had occurred in American history so large in its proportions, so permanent in its influence, and so cumulative in its effects as to represent such a revolution was the Louisiana purchase."

How could this revolution have come about under the presidency of Jefferson, when "Both in Senate and House the Southern Republicans of the Virginia school held supremacy"? Adams spreads his examination of this problem over three chapters, each focusing on a different aspect of the issue. In the first, the act of purchase itself, and President Jefferson, who was ultimately responsible for the purchase, come under scrutiny. Adams shows that Jefferson knew from the start that in negotiating a treaty for the purchase of Louisiana he was violating his own professed convictions on the limits of executive authority. "The principle of strict construction was the breath of his political life," yet he took it upon himself, as head of the federal government, to authorize a treaty which added a large population of foreign subjects and a vast extent of territory to the United States. The value of the action made it irresistible, but Jefferson knew he had sinned. He proposed that the government throw itself upon the nation for an "act of indemnity"; he wrote and offered to his friends two constitutional amendments which would legalize retroactively the sin he had committed. But immediately he ran into the kind of opposition he was incapable of dealing with, the opposition of his friends and his party. Gallatin "advanced Federal doctrine" by maintaining that the government had a right to acquire territory and that the treaty-making power was adequate to the exercise of that right. Wilson Cary Nicholas of Virginia concurred and thereby elicited one of the President's most famous outcries: "I had rather ask an enlargement of power from the nation . . . than to assume it by a construction which would make our powers boundless. Our peculiar security is in the possession of a written Constitution. Let us not make it a blank paper by construction."

There were causes militating against the path of action desired by Jefferson: the possibility of endangering the treaty, the immense enthusiasm for the purchase throughout the country which might not brook constitutional quibbles, the pressure of southern statesmen whose "chief ambition . . . in foreign affairs was to obtain the Floridas and New Orleans"; but Adams does not write of these causes as though they were adequate to override the President's constitutional scruples. In the end it was moral weakness that brought Jefferson to commit the "fatal error which . . . he could neither repudiate nor defend." In concluding his letter to Nicholas he quietly surrendered his position: "If, however, our friends shall think differently, certainly I shall acquiesce with satisfaction, confiding that the good sense of our country will correct the evil of construction when it shall produce effects." In this manner Jefferson made himself an accomplice in the destruction of one of the chief props of American idealism, "for whether he was right or wrong in law, the Louisiana treaty gave a fatal wound to 'strict construction,' and the Jeffersonian theories never again received general support. . . . He had declared that he would acquiesce with satisfaction in making blank paper of the Constitution."

Weakness in the President was coupled with sheer perversity, from the point of view of strict construction, in the Congress. In the two chapters that further deal with this issue Adams marches one Republican congressman after another to the rostrum and has them all either evade the constitutional issue or spout pure Federalist doctrine. Not one questioned the inherent right of the federal government to acquire territory. Instead the Republicans appealed to all those implied powers which had formerly seemed to them so fraught with danger to states' rights, powers intrinsic to the right of acquisition, or to the right of treaty-making. Even the war power and the "necessary and proper" clause were called upon to justify the government's action. Since such enhancement of federal sovereignty was in accord with what had always been Federalist theory, the only matter actually at issue between the two parties was whether Louisiana was to be regarded as a colony or as a territory. But this question was totally unimportant beside the fact of essential agreement between the parties on the right of the government to do what it had done independently of the people and of the states. "Whether the government at Washington could possess Louisiana as a colony or admit it as a State, was a difference of no great matter if the cession were to hold good; the essential point was that for the first time in the national history all parties agreed in admitting that the government could govern."

Having gone so far, Congress went on to exceed itself in the provisions it made for ruling the new territory, one of which preserved intact the form of the existing Spanish administration but substituted Jefferson's executive power for the power of the King. In brief, the Territory of Orleans, as it was called, received a government "in which the people of Louisiana were to have no share." Despite the shock of many Republican members at the admitted unconstitutionality of what they had done, the bills setting up a territorial administration passed Congress easily and became the expression of United States power in the new territory.

Perhaps one of the gravest lapses of the *History* is Adams' failure to explain adequately the reasons for Congress' action. It may have been that he thought no explanation possible. The tone and import of his survey of the Louisiana Purchase is dominated by the spirit of *John Randolph*. On page after page he seems interested in nothing but moral failure, the corruption of the Republicans by power and their abandonment of principle. His summary of the whole incident's meaning amounts to an indictment of the Republicans for their betrayal of the cause of idealism, and the language of this indictment recovers some of the sting of the earlier book:

> Within three years of his inauguration Jefferson bought a foreign colony without its consent and against its will, annexed it to the United States by an act which he said made blank paper of the Constitution; and then he who had found his predecessors too monarchical, and the Constitution too liberal in powers . . . made himself monarch of the new territory, and wielded over it, against its protests, the powers of its old kings. Such an experience was final; no century of slow and half-understood experience could be needed to prove that the hopes of humanity lay thenceforward, not in attempting to restrain the government from doing whatever the majority should think necessary, but in raising the people themselves till they should think nothing necessary but what was good.

With these words Adams lays to rest the doctrine of states' rights so far as American idealism is concerned. It continues to figure in the book as a point of departure from which the development of American nationality can be measured, but after the Louisiana Purchase states' rights is treated more and more as a theme of divisive, sectional politics, eventually providing the rationale of the treasonable conspiracy for New England secession. "No party could claim the right to ignore its principles at will," and when the Republicans chose to let the government for which they were responsible define its own powers, to that extent they surrendered their character as idealists and their claim upon an ideal future.

Once the doctrine of states' rights is buried, however, the *History* reverts to its original dispassionateness, and much of the force of moral condemnation, like that contained in the passage quoted above, is dissipated by a renewal of Adams' generosity toward President Jefferson's motives. This shift in tone has the effect of creating an ambiguity in the reader's mind as to the author's true attitude toward the issue of states' rights and Jefferson's part in it, an ambiguity which was probably chiefly responsible for the charges made by some reviewers when the *History* first appeared that Adams showed a dishonest partiality for Jefferson.

Such a misconception could arise only from a failure to grasp and sympathize with the subtle flexibility of Adams' characterization. As in the earlier books, Jefferson is the arch-idealist, the most ambitious and utopian of the Republican visionaries, whose every conscious act and thought in the political field spring from his practically indestructible faith in an imminent and rationally attainable perfection. The doctrine of states' rights, therefore, was idealistic in its motives; Jefferson was "bent on restricting the powers of the national government in the interests of human liberty." In his behavior, and the behavior of his party, during the whole Louisiana affair, however, Adams can see nothing but abandonment of principle and the flagrant betrayal of public promises. The duplicity, even if unconscious, and the silence with which the Republicans shifted their grounds of action put them in the position of justifying means by ends, a position more fatal to idealism than betrayal alone would have been. For these reasons Adams finds Jefferson and his friends guilty of moral corruption.

But at the same time, he has made it plain from the start of the *History* that in his view of democratic idealism states' rights is not a central or even a necessary doctrine. Sympathizing with the essential purpose of the Republicans, Adams nevertheless regards Jefferson's commitment to states' rights as a theoretical mistake. Gallatin's less rigid attitude seems to him far more sensible, namely that government ought to have all the power it needs for national ends, though it ought to use that power sparingly and with as little interference as possible in the affairs of private individuals. Jefferson himself, Adams thinks, was naturally predisposed to agree with Gallatin despite the doctrinaire cast of his mind. To Adams, the Jefferson of 1800 "seemed . . . awkward in the intellectual restraints of his own political principles." "The science of politics, if limited to the Resolutions of Virginia and Kentucky, must degenerate into an enumeration of powers reserved from exercise. Thought could find little room for free development where it confined its action to narrowing its own field." Jefferson's temperament was antithetical to such a confinement of thought. "His instincts led him to widen rather than to narrow the bounds of every intellectual exercise; and if vested with political authority, he could no more resist the temptation to stretch his powers than he could abstain from using his mind on any subject merely because he might be drawn upon ground supposed to be dangerous."

Thus Jefferson's defection from the "intellectual restraints" of his own fashioning is prefigured in the terms of Adams' initial sketch of his character. These terms make it clear that if in his defection Jefferson deserved moral censure, he also merited a degree of congratulation for having widened rather than narrowed "the bounds of . . . intellectual exercise." Here is the explanation of Adams' double response to Jefferson's conduct in the Louisiana affair: to reach out for powers once scorned as monarchical and to acquiesce in making blank paper of the Constitution are morally culpable acts, but to destroy some of the barriers of thought and action in politics is, however dangerous, both liberating and invigorating. When Jefferson moves on, in his second inaugural address, to recommend that a plan of internal improvements be drawn up for the day when payment of the debt would no longer absorb most of the government's revenue, Adams cannot help but comment approvingly that "the wisdom of this course was evident." The second inaugural looked forward to a time when one-third of the federal government's income might be applied to "rivers, canals, roads, arts, manufactures, education, and other great objects." By this plan, to be sure, "every principle of the Republican party, past or to come, was put to nought," but Adams judged that in it, "Jefferson proved the liberality and elevation of his mind; and if he did this at some cost to his consistency, he did only what all men had done whose minds kept pace with the movement of their time."

III

The story of the Embargo, which was the second great crisis of the Republican experiment, is the crucial episode of the *History* and the philosophic center of the entire narrative. In the Embargo, democratic idealism ventured into direct competition with the societies against which it had revolted. Historical circumstances forced a test of strength between the old and new systems. For Adams this situation provided a test of principle, a more or less conclusive means of evaluating the truth of democratic assertion and the validity of democratic optimism. In the structure of the *History* the Embargo produces the moment of sharpest conflict, highest drama, and intensest revelation.

"Peace," said President Jefferson in 1803 when his administration was first threatened by the possibility of war,—"Peace is our passion. . . . We prefer trying *every* other just principle, right and safety, before we would recur to war." His "unswerving" adherence to this purpose, Adams thinks, gave his conduct of foreign affairs a "remarkable" consistency. "Through difficulties, trials, and temptations of every kind he held fast to this idea, which was the clew to whatever seemed inconsistent, feeble, or deceptive in his administration." The Embargo culminated Jefferson's passion for peace; before all else, it was the fruit of his conviction that he had found a "just principle" which afforded him an alternative to war.

The importance of peace in the American constellation of ideals, and the reasons for Jefferson's tenacity in struggling to preserve it, have been amply discussed in an earlier section of this chapter. Only by avoiding war could Americans break with the past effectively so far as economic progress and governmental purity were concerned. In the light of their goal, war was "folly," and "the worst of blunders." Furthermore, it seemed almost instinctively repugnant to them in a way that set them apart from other peoples. Not that Americans lacked courage; as individuals they were willing to take the greatest risks and to face countless dangers. But as a society, Adams says, they shrank from force, showed "want of self-confidence," and feared the possibility of victory as much as the chance of defeat. Success in war only put them in mind of the corruption to be expected of a military establishment and its threat to civil authority. Indeed, the man who could offer them an alternative to war was their fittest leader.

The "just principle" which Jefferson had hit upon to satisfy the nation's temperament as well as its needs was peaceable coercion by means of commercial restrictions. Jefferson intended to protect American rights and further American ends by using the country's trade as a counterweight to foreign hostility. He thought that neither England nor France, which divided the world between them, would be so heedless of self-interest as to alienate him or throw him into the camp of the enemy. Armies and navies were unnecessary weapons; Jefferson expected that a timely application of pressure to the pocketbook would bring nations to see the reasonableness of American claims. In this device he was confident he had found the answer to America's peculiar need for a mode of resistance and self-assertion other than war; "he believed," as Adams disingenuously puts it, that he had "solved the difficult problem of stopping his enemy, while running away from him without loss of dignity and without the appearance of flight."

The immediate chain of circumstances which forced Jefferson to carry out his theory of peaceable coercion to the point of embargo need not be recapitulated here. Commercial competition with England, Napoleonic intrigue, America's desire to annex the Floridas, the contest, above all, between France and England for European domination —these were the pressures acting upon Jefferson, driving him to push his system to its farthest limit, the total cessation of trade between Europe and America. But the Embargo was not simply the effect of these causes; it was a deeply characteristic American and Jeffersonian response to them. As an implement of peaceable coercion it embodied American idealism in its most difficult and revealing political effort. In analyzing its meaning for the *History,* therefore, one may pass over the diplomatic, economic, and geopolitical causes which externally helped bring about the Embargo, and concentrate on what for Adams was far more important, its idealistic motive, the ends at which it aimed. How well did the Embargo fulfill America's wish to find a substitute for war? What significance did the results produced by the Embargo have for the cause and ideology of Republican idealism?

Adams divides the operations and consequences of the Embargo under four main headings: political, constitutional, economic, and moral. Politically, the Embargo cost the Republicans their practically undisputed sway in national and state affairs; it gave rise to a movement which threatened to split New England from the Union; and it all but destroyed the influence and popularity of Jefferson which, after seven fat years of his presidency, were at their height when the Embargo was declared. In 1806 the Republicans were in power in every state but Connecticut; Federalism was rapidly dying, and even Massachusetts had a Republican governor and House of Representatives. In the elections of 1808 opposition to the Embargo swept all of New England back into Federalist hands; New York wavered; and disgruntlement with the administration even appeared in Virginia. In Congress, not only was the Republican majority cut sharply, but party solidarity was shaken. All in all, the Embargo, in Adams' opinion, was fatal to the old Virginia-led Republicanism. When the party revived, it did so only with a diluted doctrine and with limited objectives.

The re-emergence of Federalism, furthermore, was attended by such a radical antipathy for Jefferson and his policies as to constitute a danger to the very existence of the government. The Federalist leaders convinced themselves that Jefferson was a tool of France, and in retaliation they were prepared to offer themselves to England. "The Federalists of 1801," says Adams, "were the national party of America; the Federalists of 1809 were a British faction in secret league with George Canning." The ultimate object of this alliance was the formation of a New England confederacy and dissolution of the Union. A conspiracy of major proportions was thus stimulated by the Embargo, and only the lucky termination of the war just as the Hartford convention rose from its deliberations spared the Union an irreparable division.

For Jefferson personally, the Embargo meant the loss of what, according to Adams, he cherished most in the world, the admiration and love of the people. Jefferson, he says, "longed like a sensitive child for sympathy and love"; his idea of leadership, too, "was one of sympathy and love, not of command." At the moment when the Embargo was made national policy Jefferson stood at the flood of his influence in the nation. His control of Congress was practically absolute; at the polls his strength was well-nigh unchallengeable. Yet in 1809, after more than a year of embargo, "he left office as strongly and almost as generally disliked as the least popular President who preceded or followed him." With the repeal and manifest failure of the Embargo, Jefferson was left without power, popularity, or even much dignity. During his last days in office a hitherto tractable Congress, after having "avowedly and even maliciously rejected and trampled upon the only part of Jefferson's statesmanship which claimed originality, or which in his own opinion entitled him to rank as a philosophic legislator," refused him even the power to send a minister to Russia.

With respect to the Constitution, Adams places the Embargo alongside the Louisiana Purchase in its subversive effect upon the doctrines of states' rights and limited national powers. The two measures "taken together were more destructive to the theory and practice of a Virginia republic than any foreign war. . . . Personal liberties and rights of property were more directly curtailed in the United States by embargo than in Great Britain by centuries of almost continuous foreign war." The system that shunned war in order to safeguard liberty ended by investing its government with what Gallatin called "the most arbitrary powers."

The Embargo struck at the old Jeffersonian interpretation of the

Constitution in two ways: by the necessity of enforcing it, and by the initial claim to authority which it demanded. In order to make the Embargo work, Jefferson found that he had to have increasing grants of power, all of which were forthcoming in supplementary acts of Congress. He severely restricted the coasting trade; he stationed troops along the Canadian border to prevent smuggling, and called for help from state militia to put down "insurrections" in New York and New England. To keep wheat from moving out of the country into Canada he instituted a rationing system whereby states which produced less than they consumed (like Massachusetts) were allowed to receive only as much as would fill their need. In the granting of trading permits his manner became arbitrary to the extent of placing whole towns under ban when he suspected them of a "general disobedience to the laws." In this way Jefferson's passion for peace was converted into a nightmare in which rebellion was met with ever more strenuous efforts to suppress it, and suppression only fanned and aggravated rebellion.

But more important, and more damaging in the long run to states' rights, was the accession of authority implied in the passage of the Embargo itself. The difference between Jefferson's Embargo and all previous embargoes was that Jefferson intended his as a substitute for war, not as a step in the preparation for war. He therefore proposed it to Congress without a time limit, and Congress so passed it. The federal government thereby became the supreme arbiter of commercial activity, able to make commerce subservient to national ends even, theoretically, if those ends required the extinction of commerce altogether. Such rashness in the assumption of power carried Jefferson and his party headlong toward their ironically predestined goal, which was displacement of the Federalists as America's national party. The Embargo, in fact, was secured constitutionally by the judicial decision of an old-line Federalist judge, who supported his opinion by invoking the "necessary and proper" clause and arguments drawn from the doctrines of "inherent sovereignty" and "necessity of State."

The second main effect of the Embargo, then, was once more a defeat of its own intentions. In order to preserve the freedom of private industry from government interference, Jefferson brought industry to a halt by an unparalleled exercise of governmental control. In order to ensure the safety afforded by limited central sovereignty, he extended the claims of that sovereignty beyond the reach of any subsequent limitation. "After such an experience," Adams concludes, "if he or his party again raised the cry of State-rights, or of strict construction, the public might, with some foundation of reason, set such complaints aside as factious and frivolous, and even . . . as treasonable."

Economically, the Embargo was equally disastrous, for it was a weapon that cut both ways, and perhaps more deeply at home than abroad. A predominantly agricultural country, the United States

earned a substantial portion of its income from sale of its produce in
Europe. Without a foreign market, the farmers of the South and West
saw their crops accumulate and decline in value while the manu-
factured articles they needed went up in price. At the same time the
shipping of New England and New York City was paralyzed and
many of those engaged in it became idle or bankrupt. The federal
treasury, too, was "emptied" by the Embargo, a state of affairs that
contributed to Jefferson's loss of popularity and to the chronic weakness of Madison's administration. In 1808 the customs brought in only
a few thousand dollars where they had once supplied millions, and
even after 1808 the Non-Intercourse law kept the treasury in a state
of impoverishment. Gallatin's surplus was wasted, having furnished
neither the materials of war nor internal improvement, and the country drifted toward inevitable conflict so much the poorer and so much
the less prepared. On the whole, the energy of the country received a
serious check from the Embargo, and it was a financial disaster very
little preferable to war. Since war followed anyway, Adams' retrospective opinion is that the Embargo was an unmitigated economic evil, a
third failure of Republican ideology to advance in practice the ends it
aimed at.

Adams' last indictment of the Embargo is on the ground of its moral
effect. Here too it showed no advantage over war. Undoubtedly war
brutalized man and society, but it "could purify as well as debase; it
dealt with high motives and vast interests; taught courage, discipline,
and stern sense of duty." The system of peaceable coercion, on the
other hand, "opened the sluice-gates of social corruption. Every citizen
was tempted to evade or defy the laws. . . . Every article produced
or consumed in the country became an object of speculation; every
form of industry became a form of gambling." The Embargo, without
teaching courage or discipline, created an atmosphere of meanness
and petty treachery. "Preaching the fear of war and of self-sacrifice," it
made "many smugglers and traitors, but not a single hero."

Thus, on every count the Embargo produced effects directly contrary to those anticipated of it. Adams summarizes these effects more
pungently than any paraphrase could:

> Financially, it [the Embargo] emptied the Treasury, bankrupted the
> mercantile and agricultural class, and ground the poor beyond endur-
> ance. Constitutionally, it overrode every specified limit on arbitrary
> power and made Congress despotic, while it left no bounds to the
> authority which might be vested by Congress in the President. Morally,
> it sapped the nation's vital force, lowering its courage, paralyzing its
> energy, corrupting its principles, and arraying all the active elements
> of society in factious opposition to government or in secret paths of
> treason. Politically, it cost Jefferson the fruits of eight years painful
> labor for popularity, and brought the Union to the edge of a precipice.

Finally, and beyond this accumulation of disastrous and wholly un-
looked for consequences, the Embargo failed in its main purpose of
coercing Britain and France without involving the United States in a
war. Had it succeeded in accomplishing this, the Embargo would have
been worth its cost, and Jefferson's statesmanship would have been
vindicated. But "as a means of coercion the embargo evidently failed."
The chief reason, to Adams' mind, was a simple one:

> The embargo . . . needed a long period of time to produce a decided
> effect. The law of physics could easily be applied to politics; force
> could be converted only into its equivalent force. If the embargo—
> an exertion of force less violent than war—was to do the work of war,
> it must extend over a longer time the development of an equivalent
> energy. Wars lasted for many years, and the embargo must be cal-
> culated to last much longer than any war; but meanwhile the morals,
> courage, and political liberties of the American people must be per-
> verted or destroyed; agriculture and shipping must perish; the Union
> itself could not be preserved.

Jefferson's "engine for national purposes," as he called the Embargo,
was as much an instrument of self-destruction as of coercion. Its success was beyond the range of human capacity from the very beginning.
The insistent theme underlying Adams' delineation of it is that it was
a product of unreality, and all its dire consequences flowed from the
attempt to make reality conform to a pure idea.

Such a conception was implicit in the chapter on "American Ideals,"
but the Embargo issue, by its very nature, compelled Adams to define
explicitly, for the first time, the ground of his pervasive irony toward
Republicanism. This definition emerges at the conclusion of the chapter
in Volume IV entitled "The Cost of Embargo." After adding up the
drastic failures and misfirings of the Embargo, Adams says:

> America began slowly to struggle, under the consciousness of pain,
> toward a conviction that she must bear the common burdens of hu-
> manity, and fight with the weapons of other races in the same bloody
> arena; that she could not much longer delude herself with hopes of
> evading laws of Nature and instincts of life; and that her new states-
> manship which made peace a passion could lead to no better result
> than had been reached by the barbarous system which made war a duty.

This statement means, if nothing else, that the Embargo failed because
it was premised on disdain or ignorance of the "laws of Nature." These
laws are openly equated with the necessities of survival in the "bloody
arena" of the world, an arena in which the "instincts of life" compel
nations to "fight with the weapons of other races." Adams had suggested this grim view of Nature and its laws earlier in Volume IV
when he commented that Americans, by shunning the military profession and attempting "to invent other methods than war for obtaining
their ends," were "trying an experiment which could succeed only in a

world of their own." "In the actual state of mankind, safety and civilization could still be secured only through the power of self-defence." War, or at least struggle, is the natural state of man and the Embargo, which was based on the assumption that rational self-interest could triumph over war, was inherently a policy of illusion.

With his critique of the Embargo Adams demolishes the whole fabric of American idealism. For if it is a law of Nature that humanity make of the world a "bloody arena," then optimism on the basis of human nature's innate goodness and perfectibility is the merest day-dreaming. If the "instincts of life" lead to struggle and warfare, then a weak, impoverished, demilitarized government is a greater danger than one strong enough to interfere in the lives of its citizens. If America must take up the "common burdens of humanity," then its hopes for mental, moral, and even economic progress must be severely limited by the painfully slow pace made necessary by those burdens. Confronted with the realities of human nature and history, every one of the presuppositions and ends that inspired Republican America dissolves into the nothingness of a mirage. Hence the irony toward Republicanism that is characteristic of the *History* is different in kind and meaning from that which predominates in Adams' earlier books. It comes from the firm intellectual apprehension of the disparity, not merely between profession and act, but between the illusion engendered by abstract principle and reality.

Much of the force of the judgment quoted above comes from the aptness with which it terminates the narrative that precedes it. In itself, of course, it suggests many debatable propositions, as any reference to the "laws of Nature" invariably must. But in its context it is a thoughtful and persuasive resolution of the ironic war between idealism and that which frustrates idealism, between theory and reality. This resolution moves beyond anything Adams had previously written on the subject of Republicanism. It places within a philosophically coherent frame the whole body of facts which make up the political history of the years 1800–1816. It justifies, also, the formal organization of those facts, the manner with which Adams proceeds in his selection and narration of them. Thus the *History* transcends the limits of both *Gallatin* and *John Randolph*. The former revealed Adams' lack of an idea adequate to comprehend satisfactorily the failure of democracy. The latter, though artistically perfect, was exclusive in its subject and theme. The *History* absorbs the successes of these two books, reshaping their materials into a new unity both of form and content. In its conception of the Republican movement as a struggle of illusion against reality, the *History* is able at last to account fully for the motives, events, and human personalities which comprise the story of the decline and fall of American idealism.

The best illustration of these remarks is the Embargo incident, the structure and meaning of which epitomize the *History* as a whole. In his treatment of the Embargo Adams was chiefly occupied with pointing out the reversals of intention, the unexpected and calamitous effects which its application engendered. Jefferson set out to preserve a government so weak as to be unable to interfere in the lives of its citizens. Passage of the Embargo required that he stretch his own and the federal government's powers; the difficulties of enforcement turned him into a tyrant; and the end result was a greater curtailment of personal liberty than would have been necessitated by war. Idealism thus was converted by an ironic dialectic into its opposite; a tangible continuum exists between the pure drive to realize a transcendent goal and the hard fact of tyranny. Adams shows over and over how illusion leads to action and action to consequences, consequences which exist in the independent reality of the world and are determined in their happening by the laws—economic, political, moral—that govern reality. Idealism can set these laws in motion, so to speak, but it cannot change them; and Adams' dialectic demonstrates that to the extent to which idealism is illusory—the extent, that is, to which it proposes a transcendence of human limitations and of nature—to that extent it is responsible for the creation of its opposite, of suffering, degradation, and evil.

Adams' critique of the Embargo and Republicanism is ultimately a critique of idealism itself. Herein lies a good deal of the interest of the *History* to the student of Adams' mind. Without losing his appreciation of the nobility and humanity which went into the shaping of the democratic ideal, Adams is compelled by his understanding of history to reject it as a harmful, or at best enfeebling, illusion. Its harmfulness, he finds, stems directly from its ideality. Its wish to escape the miserable conditions of human life results in making those conditions even more miserable. The conditions of life, on the other hand, represent some kind of stable and fixed order. The laws that govern them are real and cannot be tampered with; power exerted by President Jefferson has the effect of power exerted, whatever may have been his intention. No transcendence of such laws is possible. They require of the historian as well as of the historical actor submissive investigation, but they do not necessarily mean that the world is in the grip of an iron determinism. They imply simply that all action must be calculated within the limits of possibility, a possibility defined by historical experience, and that the meaning of human life cannot be located, except at the cost of inevitable disaster, outside the bounds of history.

This knowledge is the real intellectual triumph of the *History*. In his earlier books Adams had not been able to regard the failure of idealism as anything but a cause of disillusionment and of the alienation of men from the world. In the *Life of Gallatin* what Adams could only call "circumstances" played havoc more or less capriciously with the generous ambitions of the Republicans. In *John Randolph* inner corruption came to be one of the most important of these "circumstances." But in the *History* "circumstances" are transformed into an order, the order of reality, and life in the world becomes a definable, comprehensible process, whether one happens to like its conditions or not. At the same time, the *History* lays to rest, once and for all, the ghost of American idealism which had been haunting Adams for years. From the *Life of Gallatin* Adams salvaged his hero's tragic bearing and purity of mind; from *John Randolph* he carried away a sense of betrayal. The *History* leaves him with a knowledge of the hardness and solidity of life. His sympathies are not permitted to distort his understanding; his understanding controls his sympathies. Republican failure cannot be regarded as either a tragedy or an outrage, but as the inescapable working out of a dialectic governed by natural necessities. Failure, therefore, is final, and the mind of the author is at last adequately poised to contemplate it.

◅◦ ◦▻

With the collapse of the Embargo policy the interest of the *History* for the student of Adams' mind is at an end. The important questions have been answered; from this point on the story concerns only America's painful and unwilling adaptation to the "laws of Nature" and "instincts of life." Unable to find a substitute for war, the nation eventually stumbled into it, thus rejoining humanity in the world's "bloody arena." Adams' narrative shows how two complementary processes were at work following the Embargo debacle—on the one hand, a gradual breaking down of the old Jeffersonian practices and beliefs; on the other, an emergence of national spirit accompanied by new ideas of national interest and dignity utterly inconsistent with the Republicanism of pre-Embargo days. Both these processes were most vigorously facilitated by young men elected as members of Jefferson's own party, which became, in effect, the national party of the United States. The war Republicans, led by Clay, Calhoun, Langdon Cheves, and William Lowndes, all from the South and West, set themselves to make over the habits of thought and administration which had become ingrained in government, "to remove from their path the system their party had established" during the period of its triumph. Calhoun, for example, attacked the reimposition of an embargo as a wartime measure on the grounds that commercial restrictions were not only ineffective but were unsuited to "the genius of our people, or that of our government, or the geographical character of our country." "With a single gesture," says Adams, "this young statesman of the new school swept away the statesmanship of Jefferson and Madison, and waved aside the strongest convictions of his party."

The new school was distinguished, at least in these days, by an impatience with constitutional scruples and an ardent desire to dignify the character and status of the United States among the nations of the world. For this reason its members insisted upon war as the only way out of the impasse to which British-American relations had come, and demanded that government assume "the attributes of old-world sovereignty" in order to prosecute the war. Their attitude is illustrated in the bill of particulars which Madison sent to Congress with his request for a declaration of war. First on the list was impressment of sailors, which the United States had endured quietly for many years prior to making it a principal cause of hostilities with the strongest power of Europe. Impressment symbolized the wounded pride of a nation hitherto unable to protect its citizens; it symbolized government's decision to claim for itself, and make other countries recognize its possession of, all "the attributes of old-world sovereignty." The War of 1812 was hard to justify on other, more tangible grounds. Behind its inception was the necessity, admitted by a few leaders and growing numbers of citizens, to reform the character of American government, to make it strong and respected. Even if war could not win from Britain renunciation of the right of impressment, President Madison and the young Republicans thought "it might at least develop a government strong enough to attain the same result at some future time." "In that sense," says Adams, "President Madison's war was the boldest and most successful of all experiments in American statesmanship, though it was also among the most reckless."

That the War of 1812 should have proved successful in preserving and strengthening the government of the United States was the last ironic twist of the knife in the dead body of American idealism. Having neither money, armed forces, nor much popular support; facing imminent disunion in New England, bankruptcy, and military disaster, the government seemed destined to be destroyed by the war rather than fortified by it. Yet the coming of peace, a peace which achieved none of the ends for which war was explicitly undertaken, suddenly caused every threat to national sovereignty to evaporate. The country became proud of its accomplishment in fighting to a draw such a power as England. It discovered heroes and enjoyed the consciousness of strength. The fact that Madison had not fallen, that New England instead had been humiliated, seemed to give the national government a permanence and solidity in the eyes of the people which until that moment it had never really had. With the almost universal prosperity that came in the wake of peace, the President and Congress were emboldened to conceive of their functions and obligations in wider terms than they ever had before. Madison's Annual Message of 1815 advised the maintainance of military and naval strength, the protection of manufactures, and the building of roads and canals. Dallas' Treasury Report "recommended a scale of annual expenditure exceeding twenty-seven millions, in place of the old scale of ten millions," and asked for reestablishment of a national bank. "Madison seemed to take his stand, beyond further possibility of change, on the system of President Washington," while Dallas' report "echoed the tone of Alexander Hamilton." Congress replied to these appeals by setting up a permanent army of 10,000 men, preserving the navy at its full wartime strength, sanctioning a new national bank, and imposing America's first protective tariff. War had reinvigorated a government made feeble and sick by a policy of peace; "whatever evils war might cause, it was a potent force to sweep nations forward on their destined way of development or decline."

Of course, America was not transformed overnight into a sovereign state of the old-world type. Adams is at pains to show that certain of the elements of Republicanism were fixed traits of American character, and had to be reckoned with politically once more after the restoration of peace. Isolation from strong powers reaffirmed American antipathy to war, and a great though declining body of opinion still distrusted the federal government and clung to the shaky defenses of states' rights. Nevertheless, an irreversible process had been set in motion by the Louisiana Purchase, the failure of the Embargo, and the war. Precedents had been created fully compatible with the exercise of national sovereignty, and the history of four Republican administrations showed that government would not hesitate, when the need arose, to follow them. America, despite herself, had become a nation.

In this resolution the failure of American idealism is made complete. Nationhood made forever unthinkable the libertarian and peaceful aspirations of the American people, at least in the uncircumscribed and limitless forms which they had thought possible. But having lost these hopes, what meaning remained? Like Mrs. Lee after her disillusionment with Senator Ratcliffe, the nation found itself in 1817, at least in Adams' eyes, without a discernible purpose in life. Unable as he was to supply Mrs. Lee with an end beyond herself, he is similarly at a loss with respect to the United States. The *History* concludes with a series of questions that show the extent to which the failure of Republicanism was for Adams an end of significance: "What interests were to vivify a society so vast and uniform? What ideas were to ennoble it? What object, besides physical content, must a democratic continent aspire to attain?" These questions measure the losses suffered by American society in the downfall of Republicanism. In 1800 the object had been clear; the ideas and interests of democracy had been actively at work, vivifying and ennobling society at the inspiration of men like Jefferson and Gallatin. In 1800 such questions might have been confidently answered; in 1817, "For their treatment . . . history required another century of experience."

7

◄§ ISOLATION

To THE New England Puritans, history was a continuous revelation of God's will, a drama acted out under the supervision of an Absolute Director. Their writing of history, consequently, was motivated by the wish to verify God's purpose in all that befell mankind, and incidentally to draw a useful lesson or to praise the divine wisdom or magnanimity. They were essentially allegorists of history, regarding the lives of men in the world with a double vision, one eye focused on the visible fact, the other on the hidden but omnipresent intention. Nothing was indifferent to them; no event was so trivial as to be without its burden of moral or doctrinal significance. The Absolute was everywhere and in everything, creating, sustaining, guiding the world toward its preordained end.

The end of history, God's final resolution of the earthly drama, was clearly foreseen: the return of Christ to his eternal kingdom, and the last judgment of mankind. Since this conclusion was sure, the Puritans were not without a conception of progress, though it was a progress for which God was wholly responsible. Nevertheless, God had his agents, and it was very difficult for the Puritans to resist the belief that they were a new chosen people intended to bring the world into sight of its ultimate objective. There were no grounds to suppose that things must get better before the end was reached, but the human mind is often optimistic, and the Puritans, for whom the Reformation was a great step forward in the human mission to realize God's word on earth, saw themselves as the last ripeness and perfection of the Reformation. They sometimes thought they had been led by Christ himself into the wilderness; there they had founded a church government in exact obedience to divine command, "very like," as Cotton Mather said, "unto those that were in the First Ages of Christianity." They had, in a way, brought history full circle, and if the world would but imitate the model established for it in New England, there would be little left for God to do but permanently ratify the arrangements already made.

The theocratic society of Massachusetts Bay was thus a "Holy

Commonwealth" to which its members were attached with a certain messianic fervor. The Congregational system and the civil polity which complemented it brought the "reign of Christ on earth" within reach; a whole generation of Puritans and numbers of men in successive generations passionately and selflessly labored to stabilize them amid the fluctuations of the world. But ideal societies, even in those days, were impossible of realization. The story has often been told: material prosperity and its attendant secularism, the burning out of fanaticism in the failure of messianic hopes, the hardening of piety into formalism, the uncontrollable shifts of political fortune—these and other causes brought about the decay of the Holy Commonwealth. But the intensity of the Puritan experience and the lingering of Puritan social forms ingrained habits and modes of thought that gave a permanent identity to the New England character. As the dream of corporate salvation died out and the religious and civil spheres of life broke apart, turning Massachusetts into a government like any other government, the drama of God's providence became internalized. Men continued to imagine themselves acting out in their own individual lives the will of an almighty, predestinating God. For this very reason the Puritan conscience acquired a force and strictness, not to say a narrow rigidity, such as had hardly been known before. In stubborn adherence to conviction verging on pride, in moral arduousness and thoroughness of self-scrutiny, in the cultivation of affections weaned from all worldly or sensual satisfactions, in availability to the sense, often mystically engendered, of God's overpowering majesty and sovereignty, the Puritan heirs of the eighteenth and even the nineteenth centuries sometimes exceeded their grandfathers. And at the same time the disposition inevitably persisted to regard society as properly requiring the form of a theocracy. The latter-day Puritan continued to hunger for unity in the civil and spiritual realms, for some version of the Holy Commonwealth in which the life of humanity might once more be identified with the accomplishment of a transcendent purpose.

The patriotism of the Adams family, which reached an apogee in the political career of John Quincy Adams, was one of the manifestations of this latter-day Puritanism. For John Quincy Adams the American Republic was potentially, and in large measure actually, a divinely ordained society. As he understood its motives, proclaimed in the Declaration of Independence and the Constitution, the American government was founded on a divine principle: "the natural equality of mankind." This principle had been established by the appeal of the Founding Fathers, in justification of their treason, to "the Supreme Judge of the world, and the primitive rights bestowed by Him upon them and upon all mankind, by the laws of nature, antecedent and paramount to all human association or human government. . . ." The fundamental law of the American nation was thus God's law, and the civil polity erected on its basis was infused by God's will to realize his law in the communal affairs of men. America, it is only slightly hyperbolic to say, was a messiah among the fallen peoples of the world, a reincarnation of the Holy Commonwealth.

John Quincy Adams clung to this faith throughout his life; it was the only one that made sense to him and to give it up consciously would have meant the facing of a metaphysical void that terrified him. Yet, as his diaries reveal, he did face the void with a part of his mind, and he struggled to resist by sheer will the iron it forced into his soul. He had brought himself to this predicament by an irresistible logic. For assuming that natural rights were bestowed by God, and upon all men equally, it followed (as Locke had shown) that government was a delegation of power by individuals for the safeguarding of their rights to life, liberty, and the pursuit of happiness. But happiness for Adams could mean only virtue, and virtue was necessarily something to be actively sought and painfully won. Man, he said, owed not only the duty of "ceaseless gratitude to his Maker" for the rights he enjoyed, but that "of exercising, maintaining and supporting them, by all the faculties, intellectual and physical, with which he has been provided to that end." In a positive sense, therefore, the object of government, "the government of which *virtue* is the seminal principle," was to assist men in the discharge of their duties to God, to promote, in a word, the corporate salvation.

For this reason the central article of John Quincy Adams' political creed was the dogma of internal improvements. As president he repeatedly brought before Congress his grand design for using the wealth of the national lands to promote "the improvement of agriculture, commerce, and manufactures, the cultivation and encouragement of the mechanic and of the elegant arts, the advancement of literature, and progress of the sciences, ornamental and profound. . . ." There were moments when his imagination of success in this design transformed America into an earthly paradise for him. But internal improvements were precisely what Adams could never bring a divided and indifferent Congress to take responsibility for, and the states, anxious to plunder the national lands themselves, fought him with all their energy. When, therefore, he failed of re-election in 1828 and the government passed into the hands of the illiterate "barbarian," Andrew Jackson, Adams' dream of making "the national domain the inexhaustible fund of progressive and unceasing internal improvement" was utterly demolished. His private "agony" at his rejection merged with despair of the American government's holy mission and culminated in an excruciating doubt of God's providence. Since his aim, the necessary aim of a divinely sanctioned government, had been to secure the triumph of virtue, why had he been permitted to fail? "In the year 1829 scarce a day passed," he said—and Henry and Brooks

Adams were haunted by this confession—without the words of a song from an opera heard in Paris forty-five years before going through his head. They were addressed by the minstrel Blondel to the imprisoned Richard Coeur-de-Lion:

> *O, Richard! O mon Roi!*
> *L'univers t'abandonne.*

Thus the greatest of the latter-day Puritans reached the conclusion to which his ancestors had come and which prefigured the judgment of his grandson: "The people," he wrote in his diary in 1834, "must go the way of all the world. . . ."

The theory of Brooks Adams that his brother Henry in part recapitulated and in part carried out to its logical end the career of John Quincy Adams is a strikingly suggestive one.[1] Brooks, to be sure, was interested in it only because it enabled him to use his family—he almost never wrote without self-dramatization—as a symbol of the decay of American society, a subject for which he had long entertained a morbidly satisfying obsession. Nevertheless, when he compared Henry Adams in 1869 listening to the announcement of Grant's cabinet with John Quincy Adams in 1832 prophesying the dissolution of the Union, he put his finger on a real and significant likeness.

For Henry Adams had begun his Washington experiment in a frame of mind similar to, though much more heavily qualified by irony, that in which his grandfather as a young man had undertaken the writing of the Publicola or Marcellus papers. He too was the earnest and disinterested expounder of public policy according to the moral law. His stance was that of the Puritan reformer, chastising the great and the powerful for their lack of principle and recalling them to their duty. He too conceived, rather more by force of instinct that by conscious intent, the American government as a potential Holy Commonwealth, needing only to recover the true constitutional way in order to resume once more its leadership of humanity's progress. But the beginning of the Gilded Age was, to put it mildly, an unpropitious moment for the restoration of a Puritan outlook in national affairs. Even worse, that outlook itself was nearly dead, a finicking and carping anachronism too strait-laced to encompass the expanding life that underlay the moral disorder of the era. Henry Adams was not long in finding this out, nor was it for him so devastating an experience as a similar discovery had been for John Quincy Adams. His reaction was to wash his hands of politics in disgust, to turn all the scorn of a whipped idealist upon his own past innocence, and to set about constructing a larger view of American history that would explain his failure and render him morally invulnerable to any such future shocks.

---

[1] See his introduction: "The Heritage of Henry Adams" to Henry Adams, *The Degradation of the Democratic Dogma* (New York: Macmillan, 1919).

But Puritanism was in the blood, as he well realized. It was not to be purged by self-contempt or a mere intellectual decision. The great historical enterprise that began with the *Life of Albert Gallatin* and ended with the *History* shows the transmutation of critical energy generated by Puritan motives into a philosophy of American history. The faith with which Adams had begun his Washington experiment, as it lost the power to stimulate action and give life meaning, re-emerged in the form of a strenuous curiosity, the essence of which might be phrased: What had made America an object of faith in the first place? or more simply: What did America originally mean?

That he should have concentrated on the period of democratic ideal-ism, and treated it as he did, shows the natively Puritan cast of Adams' mind. For he re-created the America of the Age of Jefferson along the lines of a Holy Commonwealth, attributing to it the kind of aspira-'ion with which the first New Englanders imbued the Civil Covenant f Massachusetts Bay. That is why we find a vein of pure sympathetic sponse to Republicanism running through all of Adams' early books. Ie has not, oddly enough, usually been regarded as favorable to the Republican leaders in his work, although at various times he claimed to be. Indeed, he often seems to enjoy punishing them with the ex-quisite calamities of history. But the foregoing chapters have shown how deeply implicated Adams was in the irony he meted out to Jeffer-son, Gallatin, and Madison. They were for him archetypes of the ealism to which he had naturally been drawn and by which he too .ad been cheated.

The histories, however, were not mere acts of commemoration. The swer they provided to the question with which they began asserted hat idealism was finished in the United States and that the conditions of life in any case made such idealism a dream and a delusion. What Adams had found, in other words, was that not only had providence not been identified with the social aims of democratic idealism, but that providence was a wholly mysterious and incomprehensible force, an awesome and uncovenanted *Deus Absconditus*. Providence was His-tory itself, the mighty stream that carried men like Jefferson and Madison "kicking and gesticulating" toward its own "ultimate ocean." The determinism which we noted as an element of Adams' *History* and which occasionally took the form of a certain imprecise and hesi-tant scientism, was a reversion of the Puritan mind to its most primi-tive level of experience. Adams concedes, as John Quincy Adams could never quite bring himself to, that God has no discoverable moral intention in history, but God *exists*, as the mighty stream in its re-lentless flow testifies. And if He exists, there must be an end toward which history is aiming. The problem of the historian, as Adams now understood it, was to find a new means of glimpsing that end or at least of calculating the direction of movement. It was, in fact, the

only problem, on which all intelligibility depended. Here is the origin
of his compulsively driven attempt to make a science of history.

◄§ §►

To Adams, as to Mrs. Lee and Esther, life had no meaning unless it
served a transcendent object. His abandonment of the Washington experiment and his analysis of democratic idealism led him to the same
point reached by his heroines when they rejected the suitors who
promised to remedy their "feminine want of motive in life." Both of
these women had demanded that integrity and idealism go together;
both had chosen, when they found that idealism threatened to destroy
integrity, to salvage their own souls. Mrs. Lee could at least keep her
moral senses alive, and Esther could attend to the lesson of Niagara.
But over the endings of both their stories hangs a sense of bleakness
and loss. What were they to do with themselves now?

The fates of his heroines foreshadowed Henry Adams' own predicament with remarkable accuracy. After the death of his wife, and especially after the completion of his *History,* he became, in Melville's
word, a true isolato, a moral consciousness wandering about in a world
emptied of all possibility for moral certainty. At least this is true of
the decade of the 1890's before he set to work again on *Mont-Saint-
Michel and Chartres.* During this period, and more or less until the
end of his life, his state of mind was one permeated by the despair
of meaninglessness. His many letters, always severely under control,
reveal between the lines tormented moods of self-contempt and self-
pity, revulsion against life and a pathetic, inexpressible need of tender-
ness. Above all, he suffered from boredom like a threat of madness. He
traveled constantly in search of distraction and found it nowhere; the
Education drily remarks that "the planet offers hardly a dozen places
where an elderly man can pass a week alone without ennui, and none
at all where he can pass a year."

Nevertheless, the nineties were not entirely without their literary
activity. Adams wrote during this time a poem, an essay, and a short
book which are better worth noting as signs of the direction of his
thought than the far more numerous pages of his correspondence. The
first of these, "Buddha and Brahma," was written while Adams was
returning from his trip to the South Seas, Australia, and Ceylon in
1891. It is a discursive poem in pedestrian blank verse consisting
chiefly of a long reply by the "Rajah" to a question put him by his son,
the youngest disciple of Buddha. Asked of Buddha directly at the beginning of the poem by another disciple, Malunka, it is

O Omniscient One,
Teach us, if such be in the Perfect Way,
Whether the World exists eternally.

Buddha's answer is so ambiguous—merely the momentary raising and contemplation of the lotus in his hand—that the young disciple is moved to seek elucidation from his father who is pre-eminent in worldly wisdom and, though once an associate of Buddha, is now a Brahman "devoted first to Vishnu." The Rajah evidently construes Buddha's answer to Malunka as a negative one, for his speech to his son is distinctly hostile to Buddhistic otherworldliness. Buddha, the Rajah says, has "failed to cope with life" and so has renounced it; but renunciation is an oversimple solution to the problem of the world's reality. In opposition, the Rajah outlines a more comprehensive view of reality than that implied by the Perfect Way of Buddha.

In the first place, the Rajah holds that all existence, including the world rejected by Buddha, is equally real because equally an expression of or emanation from the one, eternal, divine spirit, Brahma. Brahma is the unity "from which all things spring"; it is the "one thought containing all thoughts possible"; it is

Beginning, Middle, End,
Matter and Mind, Time, Space, Form, Life and Death.

Brahma, in fact, is not at all unlike the divinity recognized by Esther under the guise of a waterfall. Both conceptions emphasize the monistic nature of reality and the consequent dependence of individual existences upon an underlying creative force.

Secondly, the Rajah believes that all things are not merely dependent upon but determined in their existences by Brahma. He is a thoroughgoing necessitarian. "The Rajah," he says,

is an instrument of Brahma,
No more, no less, than sunshine, lightning, rain;

   . . . .

And when his sword falls on a victim's neck,
It strikes as strikes the lightning—as it must;
Rending its way through darkness to the point
It needs must seek, by no choice of its own.

Brahma is thus more than a primal energy; it is an absolute god, the sole repository of purpose, using men in ways they cannot control for ends they cannot understand. This is a long step beyond the vitalism of *Esther*.

Two ethical deductions are drawn by the Rajah from these premises. The first is that since Brahma is omnipresent, a man may just as well stay in the world as flee from it. The aim of his life, however, remains the same as Buddha's: "A perfect union with the single Spirit." A man who leads a life of action must not fall under the delusion that action has value in itself; only as an expression of Brahma is it meaningful, and only by eventually rejoining Brahma is the actor's life truly fulfilled. But unlike Buddha's whole-minded concentration

upon Brahma—"He breaks a path at once to what he seeks"—the
man of action must live more complexly, both in and out of the world:

> But we, who cannot fly the world, must seek
> To live two separate lives; one, in the world
> Which we must ever seem to treat as real;
> The other in ourselves, behind a veil
> Not to be raised without disturbing both.

The Rajah is one who combines the Buddhistic motive with an acceptance of the world and the conditions of life as he finds them. This
double view of a man's obligations, both to himself and to the world,
is in accord with what we have already learned of Adams' attitude toward the value of personal integrity. The Rajah's insistence upon devotion to spiritual truth, even in the midst of the "jungle" of social
life, reaffirms the lessons of Adams' novels, and plots a mode of behavior by which Adams came more and more to live.

The second of the Rajah's ethical deductions concerns action in the
external world and reflects the determinism with which he invests the
relation between Brahma and individual creatures. Since men are
purely the instruments of Brahma and act without choice, the Rajah
thinks that they are likely to act best when they do so unreflectively,
instinctively. It is impossible to act with true knowledge of the meaning of one's act; therefore one ought to execute the will of Brahma
with dispatch and thoroughness. The sum of all his wisdom, the Rajah
tells his son, is in these three words: *"Think not! Strike!"* Thus man's
life is consciously split between activity determined by instinct and
the will of Brahma, and private contemplation aimed at establishing
an inner freedom through understanding of spiritual truth.

> Gautama tells me my way too is good;
> Life, Time, Space, Thought, the World, the Universe
> End where they first begin, in one sole Thought
> Of Purity in Silence.

The attitude toward life in this poem, the essential ingredient of
which is separation between the realms of action and thought—an
abandonment of action to necessity and concentration of thought
upon the principle of unity underlying necessity—was a leading characteristic of Adams' mind for the rest of his life.

ॐ ॐ

In December, 1894, Adams, who had been elected in his absence to
the presidency of the American Historical Association a year before,
sent to the convention of that body a short paper in lieu of the expected presidential address. Printed in the *Annual Report* of the Association under the title "The Tendency of History," this paper is a
landmark in Adams' intellectual development. In it, for the first time,

he publicly announced his view that the study of history must become a science basing itself on the methods and laws of the more highly developed physical sciences. What he wanted as a result was something simple and grand, a law capable of making clear, for example, "the purely mechanical development of the human mind in society." The outcome of this desire, in "The Tendency of History" and all his subsequent works on the subject, was a complete merging of history with the natural sciences, a uniquely daring attempt to treat the record of the human past as a problem in physics.[2]

"The Tendency of History" is significant as a first statement of certain basic general propositions that Adams was to explore more fully and in concrete detail in the concluding chapters of the *Education,* and in *The Rule of Phase Applied to History,* and *A Letter to American Teachers of History.* But "The Tendency" contains the seeds of all later developments. It asserts, in the first place, that historians are committed to the treatment of man as an object of scientific investigation. The method which has brought, or is in the process of bringing, order into all fields of natural knowledge cannot be withheld from the study of man himself. To do so would be an admission of the failure of scientific method. Furthermore, Adams assumes that the primary object of a science of man's history is the discovery of "a great generalization that would reduce all history under a law as clear as the laws which govern the material world." He has in mind such a law as Darwin's under which all animal life may be subsumed; it is specifically Darwin's example that he holds up to his colleagues, asking them to "apply Darwin's method to the facts of human history." Now Adams' anticipation that such a law must necessarily provide the groundwork for a science of history is extremely important because of the assumptions it reveals. Back of his confidence that a single, comprehensive law will be sufficient to explain the operations of historical reality is the supposition that reality is some sort of material or meta-empirical unity. Only a unit can be adequately dealt with by one "great generalization." The method of scientific analysis was for Adams a means of uncovering the essential unity of reality, a unity *assumed* to characterize reality; and the drift of his work prior to

<hr />

[2] Some biographical facts are important for explaining the crystallization of ideas in "The Tendency of History." In the summer of 1893 Henry Adams had a number of very stimulating conversations with his brother Brooks and read the manuscript of Brooks's *The Law of Civilization and Decay* which deeply interested him; see Charles A. Beard's introduction to *The Law* (New York: Alfred Knopf, 1943), esp. pp. 26–8. Brooks's Preface to *The Law* (published 1895) explicitly joins history to the physical sciences: e.g. "I perceived that the intellectual phenomena under examination fell into a series which seemed to correspond, somewhat closely, with the laws which are supposed to regulate the movements of the material universe." Henry Adams later told Brooks that he had written "The Tendency of History" as "a sort of preface or introduction" to *The Law* in order to prepare the way for it among hidebound professional historians; see Brooks Adams, introduction to *The Degradation of the Democratic Dogma,* pp. 96–7.

"The Tendency" suggests very strongly that he was drawn to science *because* of his assumption about reality, because he could only conceive of reality as meaningful, as having an end, in terms of unity, and such meaningfulness, whether in his own life, in history, or in the universe, was for him the ultimate value and the generating motive.

The other points made in "The Tendency" derive from and are in accord with this central interest in science as a means of laying bare a fundamental unity. Such a unity, operating according to a single law, involves "a necessary sequence of cause and effect, a force resulting in motion which cannot be other than what it is. Any science of history must be absolute. . . ." Like the Rajah, Adams moves from acknowledgment of Brahma to the surrender of chance and free will. If there is a law of history, as there must be, then all the elements of history are predetermined by the law governing the whole. What is more, the *end* of history is predetermined by its law. Since it is a law of change, and there is only one law, historical change must be an irreversible movement toward an inevitable end. History, therefore, has a meaning; it is going someplace, and when we know its destination we will know the value of the whole enterprise and of our own small contribution to it. Hence it is the first duty of a science of history to "fix with mathematical certainty the path which human society has got to follow."

The possibilities for prediction which Adams discerned in a science of history were not the least of its charms for him. We can see that by the very nature of his interest the end of history was the secret he most cared to learn. "The Tendency," however, does not venture far in this path of speculation, only far enough to provide its author and, he presumed, his audience with a few shivers of dread at what the future must inevitably hold for them as scientific historians. Adams foresaw that the ability to predict the movement of society "with mathematical certainty" would inescapably lead to antagonism between historians and most of the "great social organizations" of the contemporary world. The organizations he names—the church, the state, property, labor—all look forward to eventual dominance over the whole pattern of man's social life. But it is not probable that the law of history will favor more than one of them, if any at all, and historians in possession of the law will find themselves in the unenviable position of having to predict the failure of powerful and ruthless forces. No wonder they will have need, should the crisis arise, of "a kindly temper, and a full understanding of its dangers and possibilities"!

∾§ §∾

Tahiti, first written in 1893 and revised and expanded in 1901, is the least interesting and least important of Adams' works composed during the 1890's. Adams' own role in its composition is a curious one; he pretended to be, and actually was to a considerable extent, merely the editor of the memoirs of Taimai, the last unwesternized Arii or chiefess of the great Teva clan of Tahiti. In what are supposed to be her own words, Arii Taimai recounts the history and traditions of her clan, tells something of the old Tahitian way of life and social order, and discusses the impact of Western civilization on her remote little island. But, although the music is Polynesian, the libretto is pure Henry Adams. Not only in its turn of phrase, but in its power of generalization and wide knowledge of European literature and attitudes concerning Tahiti, the discourse of Arii Taimai reveals Adams' shaping hand on every page. Nevertheless, the editorial convention limits the extent to which Adams' mind can inform his material and only by indirection do we catch sight of the interests that led him to perform this eccentric literary task.

The temper of Henry Adams' mind during the 1890's was to a great extent the product of a strong revulsion against his own society, the society, that is, of Europe and the United States. The pessimism and even cynicism which have become permanent elements of his reputation took firm root then and remained until the end of his life to color his view of the contemporary world. This spirit is evident in his letters which, from the time he returned to Europe in 1891, are often filled with savage bitterness against "the total, irremediable radical rottenness of our whole social, industrial, financial and political system." Even "The Tendency of History" refers, as no public work of Adams previously had, to "the present evils of the world—its huge armaments, its vast accumulations of capital, its advancing materialism, and declining arts"; and both this essay and "Buddha and Brahma" end with the author's taking refuge from the corrupt world behind a mask of philosophic indifference to fatality. The idea of active participation in life had become to him a fantastic mockery. In general, it seems psychologically true to say of Adams at this time, in the striking phrase used by F. Scott Fitzgerald to describe a similar experience in his own life, that he "had become identified with the objects of [his] horror or compassion." [3] In other words, he had come to see himself, no longer in irony but in sober truth, as a failure according to the terms by which he understood success. And just as Fitzgerald, after his crack-up, said that he became "a writer only," so Adams now became a writer only, indeed the artist he was destined to become, and resigned the hope of those successes as politician or historian which he had long, however obliquely, held in his eye.

Tahiti manifests in its devious way Adams' identification with "the objects of [his] horror or compassion." Its essential story is that of the degradation of a healthy and stable culture as a result of its contact with European civilization. The Tahitians were the victims of the

[3] *The Crack-up,* ed. by Edmund Wilson (New York: New Directions, 1945).

same society by which Adams felt himself to have been defeated; that is the core of his interest in them. The whole significance of the book, from Adams' point of view at any rate, is summed up in the melancholy and bitter fourteenth chapter in which Arii Taimai surveys the effects of a mere thirty-five years of intercourse with the West:

> When England and France began to show us the advantages of their civilization, we were, as races then went, a great people. Hawaii, Tahiti, the Marquesas, Tonga, Samoa, and New Zealand made a respectable figure on the earth's surface, and contained a population of no small size, better fitted than any other possible community for the conditions in which they lived. Tahiti, being first to come into close contact with the foreigners, was first to suffer. The people, who numbered, according to Cook, two hundred thousand in 1767, numbered less than twenty thousand in 1797, according to the missionaries, and only about five thousand in 1803. This frightful mortality has been often doubted, because Europeans have naturally shrunk from admitting the horrors of their work, but no one doubts it who belongs to the native race.

Arii Taimai mentions the decimation of other islands and describes some of the diseases that accomplished this, and then continues:

> For this, perhaps, the foreigners were not wholly responsible, although their civilization certainly was; but for the political misery the foreigner was wholly to blame, and for the social and moral degradation he was the active cause. No doubt the ancient society of Tahiti had plenty of vices, and was a sort of Paris in its refinements of wickedness; but these had not prevented the islanders from leading as happy lives as had ever been known among men. They were like children in their morality and their thoughtlessness, but they flourished and multiplied. The Europeans came, and not only upset all their moral ideas, but also their whole political system.

Then Arii Taimai goes on to list the various political crimes committed by the Europeans in the first flush of their interest in Tahitian affairs, and the chapter ends with the story of the London Missionary Society and its peculiar creation, Pomare, the most cruel and barbarous chief in island history and the first Christian king of Tahiti.

To show the degradation of Tahitian culture, with its significance for the contrast between Polynesian and European character, is Adams' most important motive in the writing of *Tahiti*. But another more specifically literary motive is present too, worth mentioning because it points toward the style of *Mont-Saint-Michel and Chartres*. *Tahiti* is Adams' first attempt to capture the inner feeling of a society. In the *History* he had been concerned with the ideas by which people lived; he had tended to see men as embodiments of ideas, or as representatives of social forces which themselves could be understood in terms of ideas. But in *Tahiti*, dealing with an exotic society of very

CHARTRES CATHEDRAL   *Brown Brothers*

limited intellectual range, he turns to the substance of life, to art,
myth, manners, and social arrangements. These tangible things, to be
sure, were the only means of communication between Tahiti and himself, unless he were to treat the place merely as an outpost of Western
progress. But they also expressed to him the mind of the Tahitian people, their sense of life, their way of seeing and feeling, ordering experience and judging value. Arii Taimai's scattered rehearsal of the
traditions, songs, and social habits of her people thus represents for
Adams a new way of exploring the meaning of society. He was to elab-
orate and develop this method almost to the point of creating a new
literary genre in *Mont-Saint-Michel and Chartres*.

8

❧ MONT–SAINT–MICHEL
AND CHARTRES

Among the hundreds of letters Henry Adams wrote during the nineties, in which the decline of the West is announced with tireless monotony and only an occasional gleam of prophetic insight, a small group of September, 1895, stand out as peculiarly important for his literary career. They mark the possible birth of an idea which was to eventuate in the writing of *Mont-Saint-Michel and Chartres*. Adams had made a trip to Normandy with the family of his former Harvard protégé, Henry Cabot Lodge, and he returned to Paris deeply impressed by the architecture he had seen there. He conveyed this effect in his letters by identifying himself with the Norman builders. "I think I can appreciate Norman architecture," he said, "better than average tourists. . . . I am sure that in the eleventh century the majority of me was Norman,—peasant or prince matters nothing, for all felt the same motives,—and that by some chance I did not share the actual movement of the world but became a retarded development, and unable to find a place." A week later this conceit had grown in his mind and he developed it in imaginative detail:

> With true Norman work, the sensation is that of personal creation. No doubt Amiens and Chartres are greatly superior architecture, but I was not there. I was a vassal of the Church; I held farms—for I was many—in the Cotentin and around Caen, but the thing I did by a great majority of ancestors was to help in building the Cathedral of Coutances, and my soul is still built into it. I can almost remember the faith that gave me energy, and the scared boldness that made my towers seem to me so daring, with the bits of gracefulness that I hasarded with some doubts whether the divine grace could properly be shown outside. Within I had no doubts. There the contrite sinner was welcomed with such tenderness as makes me still wish I were one. There is not a stone in the whole interior which I did not treat as though it were my own child. I was not clever, and I made some mistakes which the great men of Amiens corrected. I was simple-minded, somewhat stiff and cold, almost repellent to the warmer natures of the south . . . but I was at my best. Nearly eight hundred years have passed since I made the fatal mistake of going to England, and since

then I have never done anything in the world that can begin to compare in the perfection of its spirit and art with my cathedral of Coutances. I am as sure of it as I am of death.

Finally, he made this identification even closer by an unexpected historical connection: "I have rarely felt New England at its highest ideal power as it appeared to me, beatified and glorified, in the Cathedral of Coutances."

After this time, the study of medieval architecture and literature seems to have become a constant and growing occupation in Adams' life. The powerful esthetic impression of Coutances and Mont-Saint-Michel brought alive the Middle Ages for him as legal and political history never had. This immediacy of response persisted and became one of the most fortunate characteristics of the "guidebook" he eventually wrote as a means of initiating others into the same experience. For much of that book Adams pretends to be speaking directly to the reader, who is present in the person of a "niece in wish," as they stand before the monuments which originally inspired the author. He is thus enabled to keep the reader's attention focused on the buildings themselves, while he evokes their shape, size, and color and imparts to them the wealth of cultural and spiritual meanings which explain their esthetic perfection. Style, in other words, is exactly suited to intention, for what Adams wished to convey was the spirit of a world as organically coherent as a work of art. That is why he could say to another student of the Middle Ages, Henry Osborn Taylor, that "I have no object but a superficial one as far as history is concerned. To me, accuracy is relative. I care very little whether my details are exact, if only my *ensemble* is in scale. . . . Your middle-ages exist for their own sake, not for ours. To me, who stand in gaping wonder before this preposterous spectacle of thought . . . the middle-ages present a picture that has somehow to be brought into relation with ourselves." The relation was effected by the most readily available means at hand: the irresistible beauty of Chartres cathedral and Mont-Saint-Michel.

But in bringing the Middle Ages "into relation with ourselves," Adams had more on his mind than a celebration of their esthetic achievements. Even though *Mont-Saint-Michel and Chartres* was the work of "a writer only," a man withdrawn from his time and writing to please himself alone, Adams felt the need to justify his occupation as more than a "literary toy." *Mont-Saint-Michel* thus became the first product of the detached and scientific view of history Adams had desiderated in "Buddha and Brahma" and "The Tendency of History." Partly in rationalization and partly in speculation, he described the book as an attempt to define a starting place, a "fixed point," for the measurement of historical change between the twelfth and twentieth centuries. Here, so he said, was "the fixed element of the equation" in which a law of history was to be expressed.

In the *Education* Adams explained the reasoning that led him to concentrate on the twelfth century and particularly on the figure of the Virgin. He had exhausted, he felt, all the more readily perceptible elements of historical analysis that might have provided a key to the necessary causal relations of history. The sequences of individual men or of societies "led to nothing"; the "mere sequence of time was artificial, and the sequence of thought was chaos"; and so, under the influence of the new electrical dynamos exhibited at the Paris Exposition of 1900, "he turned at last to the sequence of force." Adams defines force as "anything that does, or helps to do work," a definition that includes man as the possessor of certain mental and physical powers, and a variety of external "forces" that act upon man and cause him to do work. History as a "sequence of force" involves some sort of measurement of the work actually done by mankind at various moments of the past, and an analysis of the "forces" that generated, or perhaps one should say motivated, this work.

To "reduce all these forces to a common value" in order to measure and compare the work of different historical periods, Adams finds that the only yardstick available is his own mind. The "forces" that act upon history and cause change do so by virtue of their power to "attract" men, to call out their energies, and therefore the historian "must treat them as they had been felt; as convertible, reversible, interchangeable attractions on thought." He must place himself imaginatively in the period he wishes to measure, and subject himself to the "forces" that shaped it. He must feel the strength of the motives that produced action by "translating" in his own mind the "rays" of energy that pervaded the past into the "faith" that caused men to act as they did. Only in this way can different moments of history "be correlated in some relation of movement that can be expressed in mathematics" thus enabling the scientific interpretation of historical change.

It is plain that what makes the "sequence of force" theory "scientific" is its likeness to the atomic theory of physics. Adams' basic analogy is that of the human being to the atom or whatever other particle of energy may be considered its smallest unit. Just as the atom is controlled by its "field" or the surrounding atomic mass, so the human being is "attracted" by masses of energy, or "forces," in the society around him and is controlled by them in the main lines of his historical behavior. These "forces" may be of radically different kinds; in the most famous chapter of the *Education* Adams contrasts the Dynamo and the Virgin as "forces" capable of affecting profoundly the character and hence the "work" of historical periods. It is as an historical force that Adams claims to be interested in the Virgin of Chartres; and she is not just a fortuitous choice, because "symbol or energy, the Virgin had acted as the greatest force the Western world ever felt, and had drawn man's activities to herself more strongly than any other power, natural or supernatural, had ever done."

Thus *Mont-Saint-Michel and Chartres* is an essay in scientific history, an effort to apprehend imaginatively the interior "faith" created in men by "the greatest force the Western world ever felt" and presumably to assign that faith some mathematical value in the "sequence of force" which is all of history. This explanation of the genesis of *Mont-Saint-Michel* is useful and revealing, but before we turn to the book itself, the *Education* offers a further clue to its most important meanings. Why, after all, was the Virgin so powerful a force? What made it possible for her to become, in the twelfth century, "the highest energy ever known to man, the creator of four-fifths of his noblest art, exercising vastly more attraction over the human mind than all the steam-engines and dynamos ever dreamed of"?

The answers to these questions lie both in the character of the Virgin and in the nature of twelfth-century belief and society. The Virgin, for Adams, was part of a unified world view held by a society more or less united in its acceptance of that world view. The solidarity of twelfth-century belief concerning the supernatural and man's relation to it was what enabled the Virgin's attractive force to produce so much work of so high a value. This conception of the twelfth century was another very important reason for Adams' choice of it as one pole of his study of the "sequence of force" in history. The two books, *Mont-Saint-Michel* and the *Education,* are in fact juxtaposed to one another on the basis of "unity" vs. "multiplicity." The "scientific" relation between them is stated in the *Education:*

> Any schoolboy could see that man as a force must be measured by motion, from a fixed point. Psychology helped here by suggesting a unit—the point of history when man held the highest idea of himself as a unit in a unified universe. Eight or ten years of study had led Adams to think he might use the century 1150–1250, expressed in Amiens Cathedral and the Works of Thomas Aquinas, as the unit from which he might measure motion down to his own time, without assuming anything as true, or untrue, except relation. The movement might be studied at once in philosophy and mechanics. Setting himself to the task, he began a volume which he mentally knew as "Mont-Saint-Michel and Chartres: A Study of Thirteenth-Century Unity." From that point he proposed to fix a position for himself, which he could label: "The Education of Henry Adams: A Study of Twentieth-Century Multiplicity." With the help of these two points of relation, he hoped to project his lines forward and backward indefinitely. . . .

The problems of interpretation connected with *Mont-Saint-Michel and Chartres* have been amply suggested by the foregoing remarks and by the passage just cited. They may be abstracted and summarized in the following questions: What was the productive "faith" of the century 1150–1250, and how does the historian come to know it as it

was "felt"? How did the Virgin exert her force, and what was its nature? Above all, in what did the "unity" of the thirteenth century
consist? What does it mean for man to hold an idea of himself as "a
unit in a unified universe"?

The last of these questions is first in importance for an understanding
of *Mont-Saint-Michel and Chartres*. Adams' idea of medieval "unity"
was a dominant motive in his writing of the book; it holds together
like mortar the entire historical structure he created as a "fixed point"
for his study of human movement. Three separate aspects of medieval
unity are discussed in the three sections of *Mont-Saint-Michel,* symbolized respectively by the Archangel Michael, the Virgin Mary, and
St. Thomas Aquinas. The Archangel stands for eleventh- and early
twelfth-century unity of "Church and State," both absorbed in the
ideal of the warrior-knight, both militant for the glory of God who
was the supreme feudal seigneur. The Virgin stands for the social
unity of the century 1150–1250 under an "ideal of human perfection"
who was the Virgin herself and who "alone represented Love." St.
Thomas stands for the achievement by medieval scholasticism of a
philosophy capable of synthesizing man, nature, and the triune God
into an order that satisfied the ideal of an infinite, eternal, and divinely
inspired Unity of Being. Of course, all of these were parts, though sometimes logically discordant, of one whole: "Europe was a unity then, in
thought, will and object. Christianity was the unit."

The key word in each of the three instances is "ideal"; the key
concept is that of widely shared belief in an ideal capable of drawing
together the energies of society and imbuing it from top to bottom with
the conviction of meaning and purpose. Thus, medieval unity, as
Adams represents it, was both social and intellectual, a seamless garment of "thought, will and object" torn by no discrepancies between
man's highest aspirations and his common everyday activities. Socially it meant that all men felt themselves at one with their fellows in
a commonly shared sense of reality and of human destiny. No one
was an alien from Christian truth; no one suffered the modern agony
of finding himself isolated by the responsibility of saving his own soul.
From peasant to king, all were parts of the same world, and living and
dying held the same significance for all. The *Chanson de Roland,* for
example, which to Adams embodied the military-religious ideal of the
eleventh century, was the possession of no mere locality or class. It
expressed, as no poem "has ever expressed with anything like the
same completeness the society that produced it. Chanted by every
minstrel—known by heart, from beginning to end, by every man and
woman and child, lay or clerical—translated into every tongue—
more intensely felt, if possible, in Italy and Spain than in Normandy
and England," the *Chanson* testified to the universality of its ideal and
to the spiritual oneness of the society that produced it.

The intellectual unity of the Middle Ages was but the obverse side of its social unity. Not that Adams tries to pretend that every medieval man was a philosopher, but he insists that the period as a whole took for granted one basic philosophic assumption that had the profoundest effect on its character and way of life. This was the assumption that all being was ultimately unified, that the diversity and multiplicity of created beings could finally be reconciled to a single uncreated reality. If a Christian of the Middle Ages knew anything at all, he knew that God was the source and cause of all things and that therefore the created nature of which man was a part had some meaning and object. That object, at least so far as man was concerned, was obviously salvation, the return of the lost and wayward soul to, as the Rajah would have said, its "starting point." Thus heaven and earth and everything in between were bound together in a "sacred harmony." Speaking of Mont-Saint-Michel as a symbol of twelfth-century unity, Adams says it brought together "Church and State, God and Man, Peace and War, Life and Death, Good and Bad; it solved the whole problem of the universe. . . . God reconciles all." And in this reconciliation the advantages are tremendous for man. His position with respect to God is fixed; his duties are certain; his end is clearly defined; and each individual life is somehow made grand by the transcendent struggle between the grace of God and the power of the Devil played out within the confines of its own private arena.

The medieval attitude toward the question of unity was of such interest to Adams that he concluded *Mont-Saint-Michel and Chartres* with three chapters given over to a review of the main outlines of twelfth- and thirteenth-century philosophy. The materials he used here are the nominalist-realist debate, mysticism, and the thought of St. Thomas Aquinas. In each case, Adams is at pains to show that the principal issue was that of unity which the church insisted on as an *a priori* necessity and which the theologians were bound to justify. The contention between William of Champeaux and Abelard over the reality of universals boiled down, in Adams' eyes, to this issue alone. William defended unity by affirming the reality of universals; Abelard threatened it by questioning their reality except as ideas—"Unity to him was a pure concept." Hence Abelard had to be silenced and broken down for having thrown doubt on the foundation of all medieval order, and Adams, though he sympathizes with the philosopher, is inclined to feel that the Church could not have acted otherwise. The essence of mysticism was, of course, the assertion of unity even to the point of excluding all other propositions about the nature of God and man. Adams' mystics, typified by St. Francis of Assisi, say: "We are all varying forms of the same ultimate energy; shifting symbols of the same absolute unity; but our only unity, beneath you [God], is nature, not law!" On this basis Francis condemned the schools for their elevation of reason and tampering with divine mysteries, and devoted himself instead to the love of "sister water" and "brother fire" and "mother earth," those untarnished symbols of the one "ultimate energy." Lastly, St. Thomas, in Adams' view of the progress of medieval thought, struck a balance among the divergent intellectual tendencies that preceded him with a system that itself exhibits the architectural unity Thomas wished to demonstrate in all existence. In his system, according to Adams, "Thomas sheltered God and man, mind and matter, the universe and the atom, the one and the multiple, within the walls of an harmonious home."

The details of this system need not occupy us here; Adams' exposition of them is clear enough and requires no elaboration. But we may ask what the drift of his thought means: Why all this concern with unity? What prompted the creation of this image of the Middle Ages, so stylized and refined by the idea of unity? In answer one must, in the first place, draw the very obvious conclusion that for Adams unity was a value of the highest importance. The main reasons for this attitude have already been suggested. Unity, both social and intellectual, meant energy and creative productiveness in the whole field of human activity. It meant raising the level of each man's individual strength and the marshaling of all men's strength for common purposes. That was why the Virgin had acted as "the highest energy ever known to man," and why Europe was strewn with more material and artistic evidence of her power than any other force in history had been capable of eliciting. This immense outpouring of energy was stimulated by medieval unity because unity was equated in Adams' mind with the sure and confident knowledge of life's purpose. Only men who see themselves as parts of the grand harmony of the universe, who see their individual lives as ultimately significant in that harmony, are able to give themselves so completely to the work of testifying their faith and celebrating their own creative faculties. To hold an idea of oneself as "a unit in a unified universe" is to know what the end of life is and to understand, without hesitation or confusion, the meaning of every act of living in terms of that end.

Thus medieval unity, whatever its objective validity, has one point of origin in an attitude toward life that we have heretofore seen operative in almost all of Adams' works. The Christian world of the twelfth century was a perfect form of the theocratic ideal. In it, at least to an imagination primarily inspired by the art of the cathedral, the secular and religious aspects of life were fused completely. The society that created Mont-Saint-Michel, the *Chanson de Roland,* and the Cathedrals of Coutances, Chartres, and Amiens was the very type and model of the Holy Commonwealth. That is why Adams detected a kinship between Coutances and New England, why he spoke of the "combination of the glass and the Gothic" as "the highest ideal ever yet reached by men," and why he placed the twelfth century in polar opposition to his own on the scale of history. In that Golden Age the meaning of life was clearly derived from a transcendent purpose and men lived every moment in the presence of the Absolute. Such a condition, whether it occur in the America of 1800 or the Europe of 1200, gives society coherence and effectiveness, and gives the individual, like Gallatin or St. Francis, an energy unhampered by doubt and intensified by the enthusiasm of faith. What is new about *Mont-Saint-Michel and Chartres* in this connection, though it was foreshadowed by *Esther* and his writings of the 1890's, is the link between meaning in life and philosophic unity which Adams explicitly insists on. The unity of the Age of Jefferson was based on a social ideal, but with the failure of that ideal and with the increasing pessimism that beset him concerning contemporary democracy and the disintegrating civilization of the West, Adams found it more and more necessary to try to locate a meaning for life outside the limits of society altogether. Esther's divinity like a waterfall; the scientific law of history suggested by "The Tendency"; and Thomas' system sheltering "God and man, mind and matter, the universe and the atom, the one and the multiple, within the walls of an harmonious home" measure the progress of Adams' thought in this direction and the intensification of his interest.

◄§ §►

As for its actual contents, *Mont-Saint-Michel* is not primarily about society or philosophy but about art. Art serves Adams as his chief means of approach to an understanding of twelfth- and thirteenth-century life. It is necessary, therefore, to examine his use of the materials of art and his attitude toward art in general in order to throw light on the reasons for its prominence in *Mont-Saint-Michel*.

First among his reasons and most directly to the point, the work produced by medieval energy, insofar as it is still available to us, is embodied in art: cathedrals, stained glass windows, sculpture, stories and poems. From these remains, far more than from the historical record, we can tell how powerfully medieval ideals stimulated creative activity. Also we can divine through art, more directly than by any other means, the nature of these ideals. *Mont-Saint-Michel and Chartres* rests almost entirely on Adams' belief that the interpretation of the age's art is the key to the interpretation of its society. Mont-Saint-Michel and the Cathedral of Chartres figure in the book as concrete embodiments of medieval ideals, as works in which everything of value in the life of medieval society was given its fullest expression. "The ultimate cathedral of the 13th century," Adams wrote,

> was deliberately intended to unite all the arts and sciences in the direct service of God. It was a Chicago Exposition for God's profit. It

showed an Architectural exhibit, a Museum of Painting, Glass-staining, Wood and Stone Carving, Music, vocal and instrumental, Embroidering, Jewelry and Gem-setting, Tapestry-weaving, and I know not what other arts, all in one building. It was the greatest single creation of man.

Such a creation, gathering together so completely the ideas and arts of its time, was the perfect means of access to the forces that shaped and molded it and that shaped and molded the life of the Middle Ages.

It is his concentration upon art that provides Adams with a method of knowing the attractive forces current in medieval society "as they had been felt." For art has the advantage over philosophy, or economic statistics, or most historical records, in being charged with emotion, the essence of human vitality. To Adams, art springs primarily out of the emotions engendered in society by the forces that attract it; hence the historian, by responding to the emotion contained in art, can recapture the quality and intensity of society's motives, measuring them, as it were, from the inside. Adams' treatment of art, therefore, is predominantly an attempt to register and translate the emotions it expresses. He thinks of religious art as "the measure of human depth and sincerity," and his admiration for twelfth- and thirteenth-century architecture comes from his apprehension of the "depth and sincerity" of feeling which it reflects.

Adams' way of using the materials of art is amply illustrated in the early chapters concerning Mont-Saint-Michel and the religious-military ideal it represented. With respect to architecture, his method usually is to describe and give measurements in a manner not unlike that of a guidebook, to report some of the historical circumstances pertinent to the actual building, to convey a sense of the emotional tone of the finished work, and finally to relate this emotion to the ideal that gave the architecture its initial impulse. With proper adjustments, this method is also used in his treatment of literature; in either case, it is the last two steps of the process which concern us here.

Adams' first comments on the abbey church of Mont-Saint-Michel refer to its "serious and simple" quality, its "repose and self-restraint" as conveyed by the "quiet strength of these curved lines, the solid support of these heavy columns, the moderate proportions, even the modified lights, the absence of display, of effort, of self-consciousness." The impression built up is one of massive dignity and confident power. But the feeling of repose is contradicted by the ambition and restlessness also built into Mont-Saint-Michel. "Perched on the extreme point of this abrupt rock, the Church Militant with its aspirant Archangel stands high above the world, and seems to threaten heaven itself." The Norman power expressed in the monumentality of its columns and arches is also a power for war under the united banners of Church and State. Its symbol is the soldierly Archangel Michael, protector of those who fight in God's cause. The "quiet strength" of

Mont-Saint-Michel thus represents a strength of will in the readiness to exert physical force and a strength of conviction in the righteousness of God's cause in which that force is employed. Adams says that the word which best describes the Norman style is the French word *"naif,"* *naif* in its simple, confident self-assertion and in the equally simple assertion of its combined religious and temporal aim.

At this point, Adams turns to the *Chanson de Roland* for further light on the military ideal of the eleventh century. To be sure, poem and building are equivalent; one speaks for the same emotions which inhere in the granite of the other, for "The 'Chanson' is in poetry what the Mount is in architecture. Without the 'Chanson,' one cannot approach the feeling built into the Archangel's church." Adams quotes the scene in which Oliver, mortally wounded and unable to see, accidentally strikes at Roland, is gently forgiven, and "the two friends, with the singular courtesy of knighthood and dignity of soldiers, bowed to each other in parting and turned to face their deaths." The gravity of the action and the purity of feeling of the actors seem to Adams the essence of martial nobility. The verse, in its monosyllabic curtness and unsentimentality, has the force of the action it describes. "It is the grand style—the eleventh century." One feels it as one feels Homer.

Then follows the death of Roland in which so many of the elements of the knightly ideal find a place. Knowing that he must die, Roland tries to break his sword, Durendal, for "it is not right that pagans should own you./ By Christians you should be served." The sword's guard is encrusted with "the tooth of Saint Peter and blood of Saint Basil,/ And hair of my seigneur Saint-Denis,/ Of the garment too of Saint Mary," all of which means, according to Adams' explanation, that Roland had gone on pilgrimage to the Holy Land and had won the support and affection of these very important intermediaries and protectors. Thereafter he had fought and conquered as vassal both to his immediate lord, Charlemagne, and to the heavenly personages who had shown him favor. Roland feels himself expiring and "turns his face toward the pagan army" so "that Charles should say and all his men,/ The gentle Count has died a conqueror." Then he prays to God for forgiveness, crying, "Mea culpa," and pleads with his last breath:

> O God the Father who has never lied,
> Who raised up Saint Lazarus from death,
> And Daniel from the lions saved,
> Save my soul from all the perils
> For the sins that in my life I did!
>
> His right-hand glove to God he proffered;
> Saint Gabriel from his hand took it;
>
> . . . .
>
> The soul of the Count they bear to Paradise.

Adams sees in the prayer of Roland and in the subsequent action of Gabriel further evidence of the naïveté of eleventh-century society. The feudal relationship is carried over intact into the spiritual realm without any qualms or suspicion of impropriety:

> God the Father was the feudal seigneur, who raised Lazarus—his baron or vassal—from the grave, and freed Daniel, as an evidence of his power and loyalty; a seigneur who never lied, or was false to his word. . . . To this seigneur, Roland in dying, proffered . . . his right-hand gauntlet. Death was an act of homage. God sent down his Archangel Gabriel as his representative to accept the homage and receive the glove. . . . God was not farther away than Charlemagne.

It is evident that the naïveté of the equivalence between God and Charlemagne signifies to Adams a unity of spirit that was the real source of the "simple, serious, silent dignity and energy of the eleventh century." No gulf separated this world and the next in Roland's mind. The feudal code and his military instinct told him exactly how to behave in each, and his actions proved their harmony by his very unconsciousness of the distinction. The *Chanson,* like Mont-Saint-Michel, becomes under Adams' hand an expression of the central fact of medieval life. Both building and poem reach the same assured conclusion which was never in doubt—"One looks back on it all as a picture; a symbol of unity; an assertion of God and Man in a bolder, stronger, closer union than ever was expressed by other art."

There is another quality of medieval art by which the spiritual unity underlying it is attested. Nothing in *Mont-Saint-Michel* strikes the reader more conspicuously than Adams' insistence that the Archangel's and the Virgin's tastes alone were responsible for the design and ornamentation of their respective shrines. Of Mont-Saint-Michel Adams says, "What would take most time to study . . . would be the instinct of the Archangel's presence which has animated his architecture. The masculine, military energy of Saint Michael lives still in every stone. The genius that realized this warlike emotion has stamped his power everywhere, on every centimetre of his work." And even more repeatedly is it said of Chartres that there "one sees everywhere the Virgin, and nowhere any rival authority; one sees her give orders, and architects obey them; but very rarely a hesitation as though the architect were deciding for himself." "Chartres was made what it is," he continues, "not by the artist, but by the Virgin." "The sermon of Chartres, from beginning to end, teaches and preaches and insists and reiterates and hammers into our torpid minds the moral that the art of the Virgin was not that of her artists but her own."

This moral suggests the chief reason for the artistic supremacy of Chartres: the Virgin's taste was naturally more exacting and refined than that of any human artist. She inspired her artists with her own perfect sense of fitness and harmony, so that, to the viewer, "the inspiration of the art . . . proves the Virgin's presence." But Adams' teaching and preaching and reiteration and hammering into our torpid minds the lesson of the Virgin's responsibility for the artistic triumph of Chartres has another motive beside the wish to praise the beauty of the cathedral as a work of art. It is, for him, a way of saying that the creation of Chartres was an act of pure, impersonal devotion. No mere human interests were consulted; no personal motives satisfied; no private tastes indulged; one theme alone dominated every choice in planning and decoration—"the purity, the beauty, the grace, and the infinite loftiness of Mary's nature, among the things of earth, and above the clamour of kings."

In his emphasis upon the impersonality of the work done at Chartres, Adams shows exactly the same attitude toward the moral significance of idealism that was discernible in his earlier books. Whenever his heroes and heroines sought or attached themselves to an ideal, it was with the sense of needing an object greater than themselves, capable of justifiably demanding self-abnegation and sacrifice. Both Mrs. Lee and Esther yearned for ends beyond personal gratification; both rejected their lovers for having betrayed their need for such ends. In Adams' mind the ideal was always an impersonal object requiring impersonal service, and after the failure, according to this standard, of democracy and contemporary religion, he found the ideal *par excellence* in the twelfth-century Virgin of Chartres. For her sake, the artists as individuals and society as a whole showed a capacity for self-disregard that made the building of Chartres seem to Adams one of the greatest of Mary's miracles. For the artist, his reward was not properly money but eventual promotion "to decorate the Queen of Heaven's palace in the New Jerusalem," and since Mary also "disposed of hell," his interest in eternity directed him to bend every effort toward meeting her standard of perfection. As for "the people's sincerity in employing the artists," Adams quotes at length from a letter of Archbishop Hugo of Rouen to Bishop Thierry of Amiens describing the outburst of piety that brought princes, nobles, and peasants together for the job of hauling the stone for Chartres from the quarries five miles away. In the violent exertion of the holy work, all men purified and forgot themselves; when they rested, they confessed their sins and forgave their enemies; a "unity of hearts," Hugo says, was established. The utter impersonality and selflessness of this work given to Mary informed the finished product; it is "the spirit which was built into the cathedral with the stone," the spirit that helped make the cathedral "the greatest single creation of man."

Mary's power to attract the energies of men is adequately confirmed by Archbishop Hugo's testimony and by the hundreds of cathedrals of Notre Dame which are scattered over the whole map of France.

Finally to understand this extraordinary power, we must turn to the last important issue raised by *Mont-Saint-Michel and Chartres,* the character of the Virgin herself. What was the meaning, as Adams saw it, of this "ideal of human perfection" who was "loved and adored . . . with a passion such as no other deity has ever inspired"?

The Virgin embodied two divine principles from which she derived her unique power. They may be called the principle of Sex and the principle of Love. The first is related to the obvious fact that in the Christian pantheon Mary is the only woman. She is the sole representative there of sexual energy, the Christianized version of what had formerly been apotheosized as "Diana of the Ephesians" or "any of the Oriental goddesses." As the *Education* puts it: "She was goddess because of her force; she was the animated dynamo; she was reproduction—the greatest and most mysterious of all energies; all she needed was to be fecund." Christianity required such a figure because of the double nature of reality. Philosophy insisted that there must be a perfect Unity of Being underlying all existence; experience and the Church recognized the actuality of separate, individual existences. The Trinity, as the philosophic groundwork of religion, could not be bent to take account of both aspects of reality.

> God was Justice, Order, Unity, Perfection; He could not be human and imperfect, nor could the Son or the Holy Ghost be other than the Father. The Mother alone was human, imperfect, and could love; she alone was Favour, Duality, Diversity. Under any conceivable form of religion, this duality must find embodiment somewhere, and the Middle Ages logically insisted that, as it could not be in the Trinity, either separately or together, it must be in the Mother. If the Trinity was in its essence Unity, the Mother alone could represent whatever was not Unity. . . .

To put it another way, Mary became the idealized embodiment and necessarily the divine protector of human individuality, of "whatever was irregular, exceptional, outlawed," which included "the whole human race." She was another version of the principle Esther adhered to when she insisted upon self-realization as the path to true spirituality. However, despite the fact that in this role Mary was "by essence illogical, unreasonable, and feminine," she was not chaos but a unity beyond unity, a law beyond law: "She alone represented Love."

The principle of Love represented by the Virgin is founded on what Adams treats as perhaps the deepest of man's emotional needs—not that the universe be one, but that it be friendly, responsive to the fears and longings inherent in the imperfect human condition. The perfectly balanced, Singular Trinity did not offer such hope:

> The Trinity were, or was, One, and could, by the nature of its essence, administer justice alone. . . . Call the three Godheads by what names

one liked, still they must remain One; must administer one justice; must admit only one law. In that law, no human weakness or error could exist; by its essence it was infinite, eternal, immutable. There was no crack and no cranny in the system, through which human frailty could hope for escape. One was forced from corner to corner by a remorseless logic until one fell helpless at Mary's feet.

Mary provided the crack or the cranny through which human frailty might hope for escape. She could extend to her worshipers the special favor, the love unalloyed by considerations of merit or desert, that imperfect individuals required, and still require, in order to be fully at ease in the world. Nothing could be more reassuring than a divinity pledged to love and to intercede for the particular soul who trusted in her and fell helplessly at her feet. Being human, too, and outside the Trinity, she sympathized with, nay "concentrated in herself the whole rebellion of man against fate; the whole protest against divine law; the whole contempt for human law as its outcome." She substituted for these the law of Love, the only law compatible with her assertion of duality and diversity.

> To her, every suppliant was a universe in itself, to be judged apart, on his own merits, by his love for her—by no means on his orthodoxy, or his conventional standing in the Church, or according to his correctness in defining the nature of the Trinity. The convulsive hold which Mary to this day maintains over human imagination . . . was due much less to her power of saving soul or body than to her sympathy with people who suffered under law—divine or human—justly or unjustly, by accident or design, by decree of God or by guile of Devil.

In this sense of extralegality for the sake of the individual "universe in itself" the Virgin parallels and in some ways radically extends an idea present in *Esther*. The divinity glimpsed by Esther behind the symbol of the waterfall did not deny the value of the individual life. Truth, in fact, was present only in individuals, and immortality was conceivable as the persistence of individual truth beyond the limits of the individual life. Esther's god was, to one way of looking at it, a means of reconciling the integrity of the individual with a Unity of Being which gave that integrity an ultimate meaning. The Virgin is another, and far less abstract, way of asserting the moral value of individual integrity. She upholds and dignifies what might otherwise be regarded as a mere necessity of matter or inscrutable permission of God: "Duality, Diversity, Infinity—Sex!" By her love of creatures she establishes their claim to be themselves, and yet reconciles them to a Unity which, without her, would be almost too transcendent. In her "the instinct of individuality" takes its highest and most gracious form of self-assertion, an assertion not of self but of love between the divine and the human.

ঙ্গ ৪ক

The proclaimed scientific intention of *Mont-Saint-Michel and Chartres*—to fix a point from which the subsequent history of the West might be calculated mathematically in a "sequence of force"— falls to pieces upon examination of the book. Indeed, such an intention, although it provides a useful insight into the working of Adams' mind, is, in the light of what he actually wrote, blatantly irrelevant. How could he have hoped to give mathematical value to the Archangel Michael and the Virgin Mary? How could the rays of energy of the twelfth and thirteenth centuries, translated into faith by his own mind, be retranslated into numerical symbols possessing scientific validity? The task was an impossible one, and there are no signs in *Mont-Saint-Michel* that Adams made any effort to accomplish it.

In truth, Adams was led to the writing of *Mont-Saint-Michel* not by a scientific hypothesis but by the new direction of thought his mind had taken in the 1890's, in combination with motives that had been part of his intellectual make-up from the very beginning of his career. Hating his own age, and regarding himself as a failure because of it, he sought an explanation of his failure in the conditions of life imposed by his age. This explanation took the form of the contrast between "unity" and "multiplicity"; Henry Adams had failed because the chaotic disunity of his own time had made it impossible to know what success was. Society shared no common purpose; the ends of action were lost; and since Adams could see action as meaningful only in the light of the ends it aimed for, the action of his age, his own included, was doomed beforehand to meaninglessness. And having arrived so far, it was not difficult to see that all action in all ages was predetermined by history. The condition of unity or disunity was purely fortuitous; Henry Adams had had the misfortune of being born too late.

Mont-Saint-Michel and Chartres is what it is because Adams saw in the century 1150–1250 an exact contrast, at all important points, with his own time. This is why *Mont-Saint-Michel* is not true history but a revelation of values in historical garb generated primarily by nostalgia and the need for compensation. *Mont-Saint-Michel* says in effect: this is the kind of age in which mankind is at its best, the kind of age in which I would have liked to live. It stands with respect to the *Education* not as one pole of a "sequence of force" but as one pole of an inner tension, a tension which was to make Adams, despite the limitations it placed upon his way of seeing things, a fruitful and persuasive critic of his own times in the book which remains his most original and most influential, *The Education of Henry Adams*.

9

THE EDUCATION OF
HENRY ADAMS

ADAMS' *Mont-Saint-Michel and Chartres* is the nineteenth century turned inside out, a vision of life fed by an acutely critical awareness of the wants and defects of the contemporary world. But Adams was a great enough writer to know that the effectiveness of his criticism depended on the rigor with which he excluded it from his book. *Mont-Saint-Michel* is a success because it is a beautifully persuasive work of art constructed out of historical materials. Criticism is wholly implicit, its force being in direct proportion to the esthetic force concentrated in Adams' image of the past.

Just when Adams decided to use this image as the "fixed element" of his "law of expansion from unity, simplicity, morality, to multiplicity, contradiction, police" is hard to say. The impression conveyed by the *Education* that *Mont-Saint-Michel* and the *Education* were conceived together as "two points of relation" is quite erroneous. Very likely it was only when the first book was well under way, or nearing completion, that his own motives became clear to Adams and he saw that he was engaged in a critical as well as a creative undertaking. For in the writing of *Mont-Saint-Michel* Adams discovered the theme toward which his mind had long been tending, "unity" vs. "multiplicity." With this apparently simple formula Adams achieved the self-understanding and the historical perspective that made the very idea of such a book as the *Education* possible. Then *Mont-Saint-Michel* seemed an obvious and necessary first step, and the next problem, in order to round out the picture, was "the usual one of literary form": how to come to grips with modern man and the modern world, the world of "twentieth-century multiplicity."

Adams solved this problem with the straightforwardness of genius by using himself as the focal point or prism through which the various lights of the contemporary "multiverse" were refracted. Only in this manner could he run some kind of order through the chaos of his materials, which by their nature had to prove the universality of confusion, and save enough intelligibility to come out at the end with a "larger synthesis" that transcended the chaos of his own making. The peculiar distortions and emphases that make the *Education* so unique as an "autobiography" are therefore clearly the result of artistic necessity. In fact, Adams was not writing autobiography at all. He *was* writing the essential history of his time; a history that could only be seen through the eyes of a fictional character, Henry Adams, whose mode of perception brought into view the meaninglessness of modern experience. That mode of perception was Puritan. Adams, says Yvor Winters, "was as passionate an allegorist as [Cotton] Mather had been; instead of seeing God's meaning in every event, he saw the meaninglessness of a godless universe, but with a Calvinistic intensity of vision." [1] In the *Education* and the essays in scientific history which complete it, the dying tradition of New England Puritanism burned itself out in a brilliant but all-consuming paradox.

I

The Education of Henry Adams is, or contains, three things: a self, a critique of the age in which the author lived, and a theory of history. Naturally, the three are not distinct but dependent upon one another, parts of a whole; yet they can be distinguished, and the book's organization lends itself to this useful device of analysis. The *Education* begins in intense self-scrutiny, gradually widening its range until about the ninth chapter and the year 1862. From then on the personality of the hero and the events of his private life tend progressively to diminish in importance. His experience comes more and more to be a means of insight into the world about him. His attention is directed toward that world, and as his own self requires less explanation, his thought about the world widens in scope, seeking a final impersonal generalization. Chapters XXV to XXX strain toward this end, and chapters XXXI, XXXIII, and XXXIV cross into pure abstraction: history cut free from human dependency and become metaphysics.

The idea of "multiplicity" runs through all three phases of the *Education*. To best approach it, a clear idea of what Adams meant by "education" is a necessary first step. One of the most unusual aspects of this book, from the point of view of conventional autobiography, is Adams' treatment of himself as the object of a process of education, "a manikin on which the toilet of education is to be draped in order to show the fit or misfit of the clothes." Taking the position that "the Ego has steadily tended to efface itself" since the time when Rousseau could indulge in unchecked self-revelation, Adams tries to keep his own ego as much as possible out of his autobiography: "The object of study is the garment, not the figure." In line with this announced intention, his purpose in writing, he says, is primarily to assist in the

HENRY ADAMS   *Brown Brothers*

education of others. "The tailor's object, in this volume, is to fit young men, in universities or elsewhere, to be men of the world, equipped for any emergency." The centrality of education thus creates a new kind of "autobiography" in which the hero's life is far less important than the influences that shape it, and the reader is given not a private record but a guide to contemporary influences.

"Education should," Adams says, ". . . train minds to react, not at haphazard, but by choice, on the lines of force that attract their world." "The object of education [for the mind 'capable of reacting to any purpose on the forces that surround' it] should be the teaching itself how to react with vigor and economy." Several presuppositions are contained in this definition of the aim of education. First, there is Adams' idea of the mind's relation to the world around it. We must recall that in order to develop an historical generalization based on the "sequence of force," Adams conceived of man as a unit of energy capable of being attracted by powerful external forces like the Virgin or the dynamo. This conception is firmly embedded in his attitude toward education. "The sum of force attracts; the feeble atom or molecule called man is attracted; he suffers education or growth; he is the sum of the forces that attract him; his body and his thought are alike their product; the movement of the forces controls the progress of his mind, since he can know nothing but the motions which impinge on his senses, whose sum makes education." Hence Adams' use of words such as "react" and "lines of force" in his definition. "Education" is another way of talking about the attraction of external masses of energy upon the particles of energy which are human beings.

Adams' second assumption about the nature of the educative process is that successful education results in the proper alignment or adjustment of the individual to the forces operative in the world as he finds it. To "react with vigor and economy" one must know the truth about the world, know what is real and not real, what is primary and what is secondary, and then one must use this knowledge to adapt oneself to the world as it is. For Adams education functions somewhat like Darwin's natural selection; it preserves the individual best adjusted to his environment, helping him triumph in the race for survival. It tries to penetrate to the steady undercurrent of force that drives life on its way in order to destroy illusion, wishful thinking, mental inertia, whatever stands in the way of smooth, efficient action. Education, in brief, is the means to power.

Power in some form is, to Adams, one of the ultimate objectives of the individual life. Education, by training minds "to react with vigor and economy," puts the owners of such minds within reach of power. They are given the chance to ride their fate rather than be merely swept along by it. Power, as he conceives it, is effectiveness in one's actions and influence over others; it is a measure of control over the energies at large in nature and society; and it is the capacity to gratify one's ambition, to achieve the success of one's projects and undertakings. Power as a goal is in the back of Adams' mind throughout the *Education*. Often he thinks of it in a narrowly political sense because his own ambitions tended that way, but more generally it figures in his thoughts simply as the antithesis of his many failures. One distinguishing feature of the *Education* is the author's reiterated judgment of himself as a failure; the essence of this judgment is Adams' notion of success as the control of power. Had he succeeded, with President Grant's permission, in aiding the cause of governmental reform through the press, he would have exercised power over the course of national life. Had he succeeded in finding a way of teaching history intelligibly, he would have "help[ed] the boys to a career," exerted power, in other words, over the "vigor and economy" of their future lives. He failed, he said, because his own education was at fault; he could never succeed in practically adjusting himself to the lines of force that attracted his world. His "failure" was essentially a failure to gain power, and at its root was "multiplicity," both internal and external, making failure a predestined necessity.

The inner disharmony that from the very start handicapped Henry Adams in "the great American chariot-race for fame" was the effect of a conflict between the ambition "to control power in some form" and the education grafted upon him as a Bostonian and inheritor of the peculiar Adams tradition. That education was not without its own consistency. Adams wrote of himself in the Editor's Preface to the *Education* (which is signed by Henry Cabot Lodge) that "his great ambition was to complete St. Augustine's 'Confessions,' but that St. Augustine, like a great artist, had worked from multiplicity to unity, while he, like a small one, had to reverse the method and work back from unity to multiplicity." The unity that Henry Adams had to work back from was one of political and moral attitudes derived from what he sometimes called his "eighteenth-century inheritance," and at other times "Puritanism." Though he never defines them precisely or at length, there is no reason for uncertainty as to the meaning of these terms. They stand, roughly, for the point of view embodied in his Washington essays, which regarded life as governed by a "moral law" and history as tending, under the eye of a beneficent providence, toward the gradual improvement of man and society. "Puritanism" further meant, as Adams explains it, the "law of Resistance" to mercantile State Street where money had a higher value than the Adamsian principles of "Truth," "Duty," and "Freedom." It took for granted "the old Ciceronian idea of government by the best," and placed a somewhat innocent faith in the benefits to be derived from the advance of science. Adams sums up the whole position in words filled with retrospective irony: "Viewed from Mount Vernon Street, the problem of life was as simple as it was classic. Politics offered no difficulties, for there the moral law was a sure guide. Social perfection was also sure, because human nature worked for Good, and three instruments were all she asked—Suffrage, Common Schools, and Press. On these points doubt was forbidden. Education was divine, and man needed only a correct knowledge of facts to reach perfection. . . ." These were the chief ingredients of the education passed on to Henry Adams by family and society in his most receptive years. Optimistic, democratic, high-minded, demonstrably capable of producing superior work in politics and the literature affiliated with it, there was but one thing wrong with such a training for life: "In essentials like religion, ethics, philosophy; in history, literature, art; in the concepts of all science, except perhaps mathematics, the American boy of 1854 stood nearer the year 1 than to the year 1900. The education he had received bore little relation to the education he needed."

Mount Vernon Street's solution to the simple and classic problem of life was an anachronism, an offshoot of traditions which were already outmoded in American society and were destined to become relics after the Civil War. Here is the reason for Adams' irony and, in general, for the oddly humorous quality of the first five or six chapters of the *Education*. Adams presents himself from the start in the slightly ridiculous light of a man born out of his time, something of a Connecticut Yankee in reverse. "He was a ten-year-old priest and politician" whose "education was warped beyond recovery in the direction of Puritan politics." But even before his tenth birthday a "new world" had already come into being in which Puritan political principles were doomed to irrelevance. "He and his eighteenth-century, troglodytic Boston were suddenly cut apart—separated forever—in act if not in sentiment, by the opening of the Boston and Albany Railroad; the appearance of the first Cunard steamers in the bay; and the telegraphic messages which carried from Baltimore to Washington the news that Henry Clay and James K. Polk were nominated for the Presidency. This was in May, 1844; he was six years old; his new world was ready for use, and only fragments of the old met his eyes."

There is self-pity as well as humor in this picture of the world of a six-year-old boy falling into fragments, but the disparity Adams felt between himself, "an eighteenth-century child," and his age of railroads, steamers, and telegraphic messages is more than a source of either comic or sentimental relief. It is the very essence of multiplicity in its first internal phase. "Puritan" politics was a "warp" or a "stamp" by which his mind was made unfit to assimilate the influences of his time. From almost the beginning he found himself in opposition, striving against the current of the time and therefore always more or less baffled by it. His earliest education, he complains, instead of permitting an "economy of . . . force," led him to disperse it in wasted efforts like Harvard College and the Civil Law. He was prevented from recognizing the equipment really necessary for success in modern circumstances and so "at the outset, he was condemned to failure more or less complete in the life awaiting him." His ambition "to control power in some form" unavoidably came into conflict with his Puritan training and standards; their irreconcilable war within him was the setting of his lifelong obsession with the chaos of experience and of history.

Thus the Adams of the *Education* might be described as a defeated idealist almost from the start, who is compelled to penetrate the causes of his defeat in order to rediscover an impersonal basis of value. He depicts himself as beginning life with a traditionally sanctioned and unified set of goals which provide him with a clear sense of purpose and a definite historical perspective. These goals, partly because they are deficient in themselves but chiefly because they are obsolete, are soon crushed out of all hope of successful realization by the facts of nineteenth-century life. Yet the desire for power remains, and Adams finds himself cut off from the means of contemporary power by the "Puritan" stamp with which he has been indelibly marked. At the same time, though he consciously surrenders the traditional goals, he shows himself as tormented throughout his life by his inability to do without what they gave him, to get along with a "utilitarian morality" such as contented the "graceless." He remains in need of ideal ends because, like his heroines Mrs. Lee and Esther Dudley, he cannot see any meaning in life without them. This need is so great that the hero of the *Education* never really loses his conviction that after all and on the whole life *must* be meaningful, even if he concedes that his own life is apparently without meaning. The search for meaning turns him toward the philosophy of history and becomes an all-absorbing motive, and the substance of his life is given its form and direction by this motive. The structure of the *Education,* therefore, is analogous to that of *Democracy* and *Esther*. It is a quest for an impersonal goal, or at least for knowledge of the goal that belongs to history, a search for what transcends the individual life and gives it final significance.

◄§ §►

The stages of Adams' quest fall into a characteristic pattern, repeated and varied, that gives the *Education* its uniquely memorable quality. One might call it the pattern of failure; it leads, in every case, to the discovery of chaos or multiplicity in the world at large. Adams' method is to approach each new situation or each new body of material with the intention of fixing it in relation to whatever final end is either claimed or implied by it. Such an end must be assumed to exist, even if only as an hypothesis of the author, for without it understanding is impossible. Then this end is made the test of the coherence or intelligibility of the subject from which it has been derived. Thus everything of concern to Adams is studied from the point of view of some absolute criterion of meaning. The consequence of this procedure, as it happens, is to show the senselessness of modern life. At every stage of his quest, Adams finds that events and actions and systems of thought fail, upon analysis, to substantiate the meanings to which they lay claim, or that their supposed meanings are, in fact, illusory. The modern world is not only incoherent but incoherable —except, to be sure, at the highest level of abstraction in the Dynamic Theory of History, a level at which no one's life can be practically affected. The pattern of failure is thus a deliberate device by which Adams frustrates "Henry Adams' " quest for meaning. It is a way of achieving his literary purpose at the expense of his hero's "failure."

The pattern of failure can best be understood by an examination of some of its concrete instances. One of the most often noted chapters of the *Education,* that called "Darwinism," shows Adams' method at work upon a purely intellectual subject, the related concepts of geological uniformity and biological evolution by natural selection. Adams, as he tells us, saw in these ideas an effort, long overdue, to bring order and unity into two of the fundamental natural sciences; they promised, even before one knew what they meant, to lead "to some great generalization which would finish one's clamor to be educated." To Henry Adams such a "great generalization" could mean only one thing: a simple, all inclusive law of purposive change from which the goal of human life might be deduced. Darwinism seemed to its adherents exactly this. Sanctioned by the authority of science, it proclaimed not only that the forms of life evolved from one another according to natural, comprehensible laws still in effect at the present moment, but that this evolution was from lower to higher, an apparently teleological development running through all of life and culminating in man. Hence, for the true believer, evolution by natural selection was both strict and unimpeachable scientific law and "a dogma to be put in the place of the Athanasian creed; it was a form of religious hope; a promise of ultimate perfection."

Had Darwinism been able to sustain this "promise of ultimate perfection," Adams' quest would have been ended then and there. But his purpose was to show the confusion of modern thought. His approach to the matter, therefore, is a highly critical scrutiny of the evidence adduced to support Darwinian hopefulness.[2] Taking up the theory of geological uniformity first, he seizes upon its main stumbling block, the occurrence of the apparently unique era of Pleistocene glaciation. Uniformitarian theory held that all conditions affecting the earth's surface in the past could be explained by causes still observable in the present, and that the slow working of these causes in the present meant that all past changes, even the most radical, had occurred with equal slowness, by minute shifts and gradual unfoldments. In this way uniformitarianism provided the setting for evolution by natural selection, which was also supposed to be a process of small, cumulative changes extending over a long period of time. However, the chief advocate of the doctrine of uniformity, Sir Charles Lyell, himself felt constrained to admit that Pleistocene glaciation appeared to be an unparalleled event in the geological record, one requiring special and rather tenuous explantion. Lyell suggested, too, that all the data might not be in, but to Adams' unsympathetic eye the problem of glaciation seemed an unmistakable weak spot in uniformitarian theory.

---

2 The *Education,* however, presents a distorted view of what Adams really thought on the subject forty years before. In his long review of Lyell's *Principles of Geology* published in the *North American Review* of October, 1868, Adams showed himself generally sympathetic to Darwinism, though skeptical on some points. The shift of his opinion, with a complete review of the scientific background in geology and evolution and Adams' relation to it, are very ably set forth in Chapter VI of Jordy's *Henry Adams: Scientific Historian.*

Later investigation has discovered evidence of other glacial epochs like the Pleistocene, and uniformitarianism is still the most common assumption among geologists, but to Adams the gap in Lyell's argument was a fatal one. If glaciation was unique, then certain geological changes might well have been catastrophic events, inexplicable to the modern scientist, and incapable of recurring, because their causes were no longer visible or actual. So far as Adams could see, "the glacial epoch looked like a chasm between him and a uniformitarian world." To cling to the idea of uniformity under these conditions meant placing one's faith in "ultimate perfection" before the cold facts of science. Sir Charles Lyell, Adams is so bold to say, may have let his wish "to assume unity from the start" lead him into the devious paths of sophistry in search of an explanation for the glacial period, but Henry Adams would not be so deluded into heaven.

The theory of evolution receives similar treatment at Adams' hands. He tells of asking Lyell, who was a frequent visitor at the American Legation in London during the Civil War years, for "some single figure to illustrate the Law of Natural Selection." Sir Charles is then supposed to have replied that "certain forms, like *Terebratula,* appeared to be identical from the beginning to the end of geological time." Where then, protests Adams—whether to Lyell directly he does not say—is evolution? In the Terebratula's excessive constancy of form, what evidence is there of anything having been naturally selected? Turning from this impasse at the starting point of evolution, Adams next inquires about its end, man, or at least the class of vertebrates to which man belongs. Where do the vertebrates originate? The answer to this question again leads to the apparent breakdown of theory. For Adams finds that the first vertebrate was "a very respectable fish," Pteraspis by name, "a cousin of the sturgeon," who appears whole and complete in the Silurian epoch without a trace of more rudimentary vertebrate ancestry. Thus forms of life seemed, on the one hand, to have remained static throughout their careers, untouched by the universal selective process, and on the other to have emerged suddenly without prior evolutionary warning of their arrival. One could only conclude that here was an "Evolution that did not evolve; Uniformity that was not uniform; and Selection that did not select."

As a result of this critique, Adams decides that Darwinism is, after all, religion like any other religion, depending for its satisfactoriness as explanation upon a prior disposition to be convinced. Its claim to give life meaning as a slow progress toward perfection is nothing but "inference, precisely like the inference of Paley, that if one found a watch, one inferred a maker." Science thereby stands accused of the same bad motive as formerly belonged to the theologies which it has displaced: willingness to ignore recalcitrant complexity in its haste to achieve unity and coherence. Since science's whole case against theology is founded on its greater respect for the facts of nature, this is, in Adams' eyes, a very damning position for Darwinism to find itself in. Nevertheless, having placed Darwinism in this position, Adams says he concluded to entertain the theory as a means of keeping in step with his time. For himself, "He was a Darwinian for fun," but "the young men whose lives were cast in the generation between 1867 and 1900" took evolution to be "Law," and being one of them, "he would force himself to follow wherever it led."

The failure of Darwinism to provide the "great generalization" for which Adams was looking is one proof to his mind of the chaos of nineteenth-century thought. As he understood it, Darwinism was an assertion of philosophic unity based on the methods of science. It was this scientific character that made the assertion of unity peculiarly of and for the time; nothing else would have satisfied the young men of the generation between 1867 and 1900. Science alone had the prestige, the intellectual respectability, to reaffirm unity in a convincing manner. Yet the science of Lyell and Darwin was bad, charged with assumptions it could not verify and guilty of dealing cavalierly with the facts it was supposed to explain. Since they were not explained, however, the facts implied a probable state of chaos in nature; but whether or not this was so, they certainly implied the failure of Darwinian science. If Darwinism could not handle the material it was designed to handle; if the method in which the modern consciousness found its peculiar and best realization broke down before the complexity of its data, then one could only judge the thought of the time confused and incapable of leading toward a resolution of the quest for meaning. Looking backward down the vista of supposed evolution, Adams recognizes the Pteraspis, henceforth his private symbol for the "complexity [that] precedes evolution," grinning "horribly from the closed entrance."

◆◆ ◆◆

A more judicious and effective use of the pattern of failure, in a different realm of experience, follows immediately after the chapter on Darwinism in three chapters and part of a fourth concerning Adams' attempt to establish himself as a reforming journalist in Washington. We have already examined this period of his literary career and tried to assess its meaning for his intellectual development; it is especially interesting to see how Adams himself treats the same material in working out his theme of "multiplicity." What is more, Adams understood American politics, as he did not Darwinian science, with an almost professional astuteness. In scientific matters, although he was fascinated by them, he was never more than a highly sophisticated dilettante. He was impatient of scientific method as practiced in the laboratory, and his criticism of Darwinism is shamelessly unscientific in its weighting and manipulation of the evidence. But in the field of politics Adams was at home. Family tradition, personal experience, and the historian's broad acquaintance with underlying motives, issues, and social forces, all contributed to make him particularly sensitive to the implications of events in the political arena. That is why the sections of the *Education* dealing with diplomacy and politics have long been the most interesting to its readers. Not only do they exhibit his superb narrative art, but they possess the immediacy and subtlety of knowledge that is both firsthand and carefully considered. In summarizing his experiences as a journalistic novice in Washington during the years 1868–1870, Adams manages to convey an idea of the situation in which he found himself that is far more credible, and philosophically more in earnest, than the picture of himself as a Darwinian nipped in the bud. And his sharply phrased attitude of disgust with the politics of the Age of Grant is persuasive to a degree never approached by all his harping on glaciation, Pteraspis, and Terebratula.

Adams begins the history of his unsuccessful political campaign by touching once more on the theme, so persistently expressive of his idea of himself in the *Education,* of his chronic remoteness from the actualities of American life. Returning in 1868 from seven years in England, he found the country, in the aftermath of war, changed more than ever in the direction first adumbrated by the steamship, telegraph, and railroad of 1844. In the last ten years a "revolution" had occurred; these years "had given to the great mechanical energies—coal, iron, steam—a distinct superiority in power over the old industrial elements—agriculture, handwork, and learning." America was bent on developing these energies in order to make the continent habitable, an immense and all-absorbing task; but the Henry Adams who belonged to the eighteenth century, whose world of agriculture, handwork, and learning "was dead," could only feel himself now more than ever excluded from the mainstream of American life. "He had become estray; a flotsam or jetsam of wreckage; a belated reveller, or a scholar-gipsy like Matthew Arnold's." For purposes of adjustment to the America of 1868 his very Americanism seemed to him more of a clog than an advantage. He was like the Indians and buffaloes who "had been ejected from their heritage by his own people." The only way to give himself heart for the effort to recommence life in this new world was to insist that in having been ejected "he was not himself at fault. The defeat was not due to him, nor yet to any superiority of his rivals. He had been unfairly forced out of the track, and must get back into it as best he could."

The method by which he hoped to get into the track was free lance political journalism in Washington. Adams writes as though the Washington experiment was a reluctant choice, forced on him by the poor organization of good society's "labor market." But gradually and, as it were, diffidently, his purposes begin to emerge. As we have seen, power for him was inevitably qualified by "Puritan" standards, which is to say that it required moral justification. He could not conceive of himself wanting power for its own sake; there must be a goal giving meaning to power, and a sanction under which its use remained strictly impersonal. This sanction he found, as his forefathers had always grimly insisted they found it, in the national good; and the immediate goal, as he saw it, was the reform of a governmental organization grown unwieldy and corrupt as a result of its fumbling attempts to keep up with the demands made upon it by war and national expansion. His task was that of "bringing the Government back to regular practices, and of restoring moral and mechanical order to administration."

> The whole government, from top to bottom, was rotten with the senility of what was antiquated and the instability of what was improvised. The currency was only one example; the tariff was another; but the whole fabric required reconstruction as much as in 1789, for the Constitution had become as antiquated as the Confederation. Sooner or later a shock must come, the more dangerous the longer postponed. The Civil War had made a new system in fact; the country would have to reorganize the machinery in practice and theory.

By linking reform to journalism Adams intended to satisfy his ambition, his scruples, and his craving for a meaningful life. What was more, in 1868 he felt himself part of an advancing tide. The "chaos" of the last days of the Johnson administration was of the sort that "often breeds life, when order breeds habit." Washington was full of young men like himself who were "greedy for work, eager for reform, energetic, confident, capable," and they were not alone, for "most of the press, and much of the public, especially in the West shared their ideas." They rallied to the standards of currency reform and the resumption of specie payment, free trade and the breaking down of oppressive tariffs, a nonpolitical civil service, reduction of the power of the Senate and strengthening of the executive, and a cleansing of party organizations to free them from a corrupt dependency on wealthy special interests. All they needed to bring out of the chaos a new and improved order was a leader anxious like themselves to "raise the character of government." And they thought they had found him: "At least four-fifths of the American people—Adams among the rest—had united in the election of General Grant to the Presidency, and probably had been more or less affected in their choice by the parallel they felt between Grant and Washington. Nothing could be more obvious. Grant represented order. He was a great soldier, and the soldier always represented order."

At this point in Adams' narrative we may pause to observe the artistry with which he has prepared for the story's inevitable denouement. The scene has been set and all the characters are in their places waiting for Grant's arrival on the stage. This arrival has been made crucial to a whole set of interlocking expectations. The personal ambition of Henry Adams, the cause of reform, the national welfare—all hinge on the unknown quantity of Grant's leadership. In effect, the meaning of politics itself is at stake. For Grant has the power to demonstrate that the national life is purposeful; that progress on a large scale can be made; and that the efforts of those seeking to encourage progressive movement and to illuminate its path are useful in the day-to-day political struggle. The "Darwinian for fun" sees, also, a concrete test of evolutionary optimism in Grant's response to the need for reform. The government must be able to adapt itself to new conditions of life if it is to survive and flourish. Progress can help prove evolution, and together they can end the quest for meaning which was the original motive of Adams' political involvement.

Largely as a result of this skillful management, Grant's arrival on the Washington scene is perhaps the best-remembered moment in the *Education*. Adams gives the new President's announcement of his cabinet the force of a hammer blow:

> To the end of his life, he wondered at the suddenness of the revolution which actually, within five minutes, changed his intended future into an absurdity so laughable as to make him ashamed of it. He was to hear a long list of Cabinet announcements not much weaker or more futile than that of Grant, and none of them made him blush, while Grant's nominations had the singular effect of making the hearer ashamed, not so much of Grant, as of himself. He had made another total misconception of life—another inconceivable false start. . . . He knew, without absolutely saying it, that Grant had cut short the life which Adams had laid out for himself in the future. After such a miscarriage, no thought of effectual reform could revive for at least one generation, and he had no fancy for ineffectual politics.

The cabinet appointees, it need hardly be said, were nearly all men indifferent or hostile to the cause of reform. However, though Adams' reaction to the announcement of their names would appear to have been conclusive, he says that he was still willing to postpone final judgment of Grant himself. Grant's motives might yet be good. Perhaps his nominations were more the result of ignorance and incompetence than lack of concern for the necessities of reform. "A great soldier might be a baby politician." But researches on this subject led to a quick end of hope. From Badeau, a friend, biographer, and former aide of Grant, he learned that to the men around him "Grant appeared as an intermittent energy, immensely powerful when awake, but passive and plastic in repose. . . . They could never measure his character or be sure when he would act. They could never follow a mental process in his thought. They were not sure that he did think." With an

acuteness comparable to that of his portraits in the *History,* Adams
sums Grant up as a "pre-intellectual, archaic" type, one of those men
"whose energies were the greater, the less they wasted on thought;
men who sprang from the soil to power; apt to be distrustful of themselves and of others; shy; jealous; sometimes vindictive; more or less
dull in outward appearance; always needing stimulants; but for
whom action was the highest stimulant—the instinct of fight. Such men
were forces of nature, energies of the prime, like the Pteraspis. . . ."
Faced with a character like this, sluggish, unthinking, brilliant in action only when the "instinct of fight" was aroused, what chance did the
unexciting struggle for governmental reform have? Grant "fretted and
irritated" Adams by his lack of every quality that the political situation demanded. At this moment of history his emergence as a leader
made no sense; it was "a defiance of first principles." Grant "had no
right to exist. He should have been extinct for ages. . . . That, two
thousand years after Alexander the Great and Julius Caesar, a man
like Grant should be called—and should actually and truly be—the
highest product of the most advanced evolution, made evolution ludi-
crous. . . . The progress of evolution from President Washington to
President Grant, was alone evidence enough to upset Darwin."

Whether or not Darwin was upset, Henry Adams certainly was. The
unfolding of Grant's first year in office was for him a succession of
disasters. Grant's temper encouraged "a policy of drift," leaving Adams
with nothing to support and the various personalities of government
and press with no one to obey. A general "dissolution of ties in every
direction" set in; "scarcely a newspaper in the country kept discipline"; and "the Senate Chamber became again a scene of irritated
egotism that passed ridicule." Adams' chief political allies, who might
have preserved for him some field of action, were caught in the drift,
or quarreled among themselves, or were driven from the government.
And crowning all this anarchy was the "famous, classical attempt of
Jay Gould to corner gold in September, 1869," an operation which
looked to Adams as though Grant himself had had a part in it, know-
ingly or unknowingly. To one who had committed his future to progress and evolution, all that could now be foreseen was "a life of
wasted energy, sweeping the stables of American society clean of the
endless corruption which . . . Washington was quite certain to breed."

As he remembers it after almost forty years, the Grant administration brought home two truths to Henry Adams' mind. The first was
that morality is irrelevant to contemporary politics; Puritan standards
lead to exclusion and impotence rather than to authority and strength.
"For one law . . . rule[s] all others—masses of men invariably follow interests in deciding morals." The morality that scruples against
the claims of interest, faction, or ambition is "a private and costly
luxury." The second truth Adams learned was that the adjustment of

the American government to modern industrial life is impossible. After the failure of post-Civil War reform, "nine-tenths of men's political energies must henceforth be wasted on expedients to piece out—to patch—or, in vulgar language, to tinker—the political machine as often as it broke down. . . . As a machine, it was, or soon would be, the poorest in the world—the clumsiest—the most inefficient." The sum of the matter was that "the moral law had expired—like the Constitution." "Every hope or thought which had brought Adams to Washington proved to be absurd." It was time to leave.

Adams' handling of this entire incident leads unrelentingly to one conclusion: the necessity of his failure due to the social, intellectual, and moral chaos of politics. Reform was based on the assumption that unity could be imposed upon multiplicity, that politics could be given order by common sense and the recognition of moral truth. There should have been an end toward which all the activity of government tended. If not, what was there but aimless struggle and directionless change having no meaning for the individual or the collective life?

Multiplicity was apparent in the failure of American society to attack or even to recognize its problems after the war. It needed at the very least a "working political system," a machine able to carry on its public business without obstructing its chosen course of development, whatever that might be. Otherwise, there was nothing to look forward to but "an eternity of Grants, or even of Garfields or of Conklings or of Jay Goulds" and such an eternity "refused to be conceived as possible." The American people might be able to carry on their "bare and toiling shoulders . . . the load of every social or political stupidity," but for how long, and why? The attainment of a "working political system" was a practical matter of adjusting means to purpose; did not Adams' failure as a reformer of the political system imply that society was utterly confused as to its purpose, or that perhaps it had no purpose at all? Here was a state of chaos that "drove the student of civilized man to despair." Men sought power but did not know what to do with it; the nation created energy but did not know how to control it; society plunged onward, carrying its load of stupidity, but knew not where it was going and seemed hardly to care. The moral for Adams was clear: chaos ruled in politics as in biology and geology. His attempt to locate a meaning for his life in the process of social evolution had failed—evolution did not evolve; and once more education had resulted only in the confirmation of his ignorance.

The pattern of failure that dominates the form and tone of the first three-fifths of the *Education* culminates Adams' use of a theme which was present in his work from the very beginning. In the *Life of Albert Gallatin* Adams had treated Gallatin, somewhat tentatively, as a failure in his endeavor to realize an ideal political system. Gallatin was defeated by a combination of unlucky circumstance and human limita-

tion; and not long after, Adams showed the entire Republican movement going down to a similar defeat, crushed by political realities that
rendered its idealism impotent. In his novels Adams engaged both of
his principal characters in a quest for meaning; both ended in failure
and the abandonment of false ideals. The pattern of failure, or of
quest ending in failure, is, in short, the basic pattern of all of Adams'
books except *Mont-Saint-Michel and Chartres*. It embodies the quin-
tessential drama of his mind. Adams began, like many another in the
nineteenth century—Melville, for one—with an inner compulsion to
find a substantial ground of moral value outside of himself: in society,
in nature, in history. Without believing in God, he yet demanded that
such value have an absolute sanction based on an ideal or transcendent
reality. Only absolute truth could give meaning to the chaotic experience of life. Only an absolute reality could provide a foundation on
which to stand in order to judge the direction and purpose of life. But
the quest of the Absolute led down to an unfathomable abyss; like
Melville, Adams was drawn by his obsession farther and farther into
a moral and intellectual confusion terminating in despair, rejection of
the world, and alienation from society. At the end of the quest lay the
"heartless voids and immensities of the universe," a phrase of Melville's that aptly describes the "larger synthesis" of the "Dynamic
Theory of History" which concludes the *Education,* as well as the
Rule of Phase and *Letter to American Teachers of History.* In these
last works Adams completes his education, confronting "a dumb blank-
ness, full of meaning."

But there is another side to the *Education,* its heroic side. In the
brilliance and intellectual daring of the quest itself, Adams converts
failure into heroism. What else gives the *Education* its right to claim
a place among the masterpieces of American literature? The *Education* is one of those books in which a man charts unexplored territory,
in which he risks seeming a perfect fool to his most sympathetic contemporaries and a madman to posterity. What Adams did was to subject his age, and in particular the historical formulas of his age, to a
new and searching kind of criticism. It was a criticism that originated
in the Puritan mode of perception—the inverted allegorical mode of
the disbelieving Calvinist—and its daring consists in the opening up
of innumerable perspectives of ambiguity, or "multiplicity," behind
the generalizations and assumptions that passed for truth in the world
at large. "By proclaiming himself to be a failure," writes one critic,

—by so labelling all of his impressive achievements—Adams out-
witted expectations and implied that no one had really encountered
success, that his contemporaries were far from triumphant, that it was
rash to consider the time of his lifespan as one of equilibrium and fulfillment for American politics and statesmanship. In placing in a wider
context the manners and formulas of an America which had yet to

come of age, he perceived characteristics to which his compatriots were blind. He saw complexities where others saw simplicities, challenging the prevailing definition of practicality and efficiency, the formula of progress, the belief in inevitable victory, the faith in the necessary destiny of American democracy.[3]

Insofar as the theme of "multiplicity" is a challenge to the easy, the satisfying, and the false; insofar as it compels the mind of the reader to entertain a difficult and unresolvable view of reality; insofar as it creates a permanent disturbance in, and requires a permanent readjustment of, American self-consciousness, *The Education of Henry Adams* is much more than a cosmic blind alley, but an enduring and invigorating work of art. And insofar as it is this, it is an act of superlative integrity. Amidst the wreck of disintegrating certainties, and exquisitely aware of his absurdity in the eyes of the world, Adams clung to the one value which all his books in one way or another celebrated: the truth of his own vision. United with an historian's subtlety and an artist's shaping power, this truth makes the *Education* a great and unique accomplishment.

II

I have reserved the historical theory that concludes the *Education* for separate treatment because it is as much a part of Adams' succeeding work as it is of the *Education*. Within two years of the first, private printing of the *Education* he wrote *The Rule of Phase Applied to History* and *A Letter to American Teachers of History*.[4] These two short books continue the vein of theorizing begun in the last chapters of the *Education,* and both propriety and convenience suggest that all three may be dealt with together, especially since we are unconcerned with the differences and contradictions among them. The three versions of Adams' final historical theory may be thought of as having the same relation to the bulk of the *Education* as do the last chapters alone.

The "Dynamic Theory of History," the *Rule,* and the *Letter* comprise a solution to the quest for meaning which is the main object of the *Education.* They represent the attainment of unity in a manner foreshadowed by "The Tendency of History" written more than ten years before the *Education* was begun. Having failed to establish unity within the limits of his own experience or within the range of his practical ideas, Adams turned to science as a way of fixing a meaning for all of history and hence, by indirection, for his own apparently pointless life. Science promised, in "The Tendency of History," to make

[3] Henry S. Kariel, "The Limits of Social Science: Henry Adams' Quest for Order," *American Political Science Review,* L (1956), 1074-92.
[4] Both included in Henry Adams, *The Degradation of the Democratic Dogma,* ed. by Brooks Adams (New York: Macmillan, 1919).

available a "great generalization" by which the facts of history were to be harmonized with the facts of nature and thus made orderly, coherent, and purposeful. The only thing that could nail history down once and for all was a law based on ultimate physical reality, a law that included every phenomenon of nature—microscopic, historical, and even macroscopic. What he wanted, Adams says in the *Education,* was "a historical formula that should satisfy the conditions of the stellar universe."

"The Tendency of History" comes to complete, if somewhat be-wilderingly inconsistent, fruition in "The Dynamic Theory," the *Rule* and the *Letter.* They are the final merging of history and natural sci-ence, the result of Adams' long meditated project to read human his-tory in terms of "the conditions of the stellar universe." Inconsistencies aside, there are five respects in which all three works, in ways relevant to this study, are fundamentally similar. I will take these points up in a logical order, rather than try to follow and coordinate Adams' vari-ous schemes of development.

First, "The Dynamic Theory," the *Rule,* and the *Letter* are all based on laws drawn from the physical sciences. In his latest work Adams refuses to distinguish between the matter of history and the matter of natural science. Physics and chemistry, which write the ground rules for science, must provide an historical method. They are assumed to be the only disciplines that seriously confront the only reality—of which history is a part; and the truths which they have accepted as necessary to the description of physical reality are assumed to be equally valid for history.

"The Dynamic Theory," for example, involves a kind of psycho-logical tropism in which the forces of nature irresistibly "attract" the considerably weaker forces of human beings. This is the idea on which Adams based his theory of the change from thirteenth-century unity to twentieth-century multiplicity, and it is actually the least "scien-tific" of his latest formulas since it depends on an analogy rather than a complete fusion of history with physics. The analogy is that be-tween a man in nature and an atom in its field: "The sum of force [Nature] attracts; the feeble atom or molecule called man is at-tracted; he suffers education or growth; he is the sum of the forces that attract him; his body and his thought are alike their product; the movement of the forces controls the progress of his mind, since he can know nothing but the motions which impinge on his senses, whose sum makes education." Presumably, if all these forces could be meas-ured, then the progress of man's mind, past and future, would be mathematically calculable. This would convert the analogy into a true scientific theory, but the hope of such measurement is obviously vain, and the historical scheme worked out in the last chapters of the *Education,* though brilliant in some of its details, is exceedingly arbitrary and unsystematic. Reduced as nearly as possible to a formula, it comes out like this:

> As far as one ventured to interpret actual science, the mind had thus far adjusted itself by an infinite series of infinitely delicate adjustments forced on it by the infinite motion of an infinite chaos of motion [i.e. Nature]; dragged at one moment into the unknowable and unthinkable, then trying to scramble back within its senses and to bar the chaos out, but always assimilating bits of it. . . .

Thus the "law of reaction between force and force—between mind and nature"—placed history within the iron grip of a simple mechanical process, but one that made its constituent values so difficult of assignment that the process could only be interpreted unscientifically.

The *Rule* pushed the atomic analogy closer to science by setting it in the framework of the "law of phase" which now seemed to Adams "the latest and largest of possible generalizations" lying on the "horizon of science." Willard Gibbs had formulated the law of phase as a description of the behavior of matter under varying conditions of temperature and pressure. Adams, substituting his own variables—attraction and acceleration—for those of Gibbs, thought that the phase rule could be used equally to describe the major changes of history. Just as ice turns, under exactly definable conditions, to water, then to vapor, so history, responding to comparable conditions, had seen human thought shift from the Religious phase to the Mechanical and then to the Electrical. Each phase represents a change in the relation of thought to nature, a change parallel to the solution of matter which, as it moves from one phase to another, becomes more and more rarefied and finally loses its identity in the ultimate ocean of atoms. The *Rule* is thus more scientific than "The Dynamic Theory" since it treats thought as wholly material and defines thought-change in terms of a recognizable law of matter. But it does not tell us how to discriminate thought-matter from other kinds of matter, or why it should obey irreversibly a law which is reversible everywhere else in nature.

The *Letter* is Adams' most successful linking of history and science. Here he abandons the old terminology of "force," "attraction," "acceleration," "phase," etc., and takes an entirely new tack. The central propositions of the *Letter* are that human life is a form of vital energy and that vital energy is a form of physical energy. Human life, therefore, is subject to the laws governing physical energy, the most important of which is, in Adams' eyes, the second law of thermodynamics. According to this law, the energy of the universe is constantly being dissipated as heat; once dissipated it is irrecoverable in a form capable of doing work except at the expense of an even greater quantity of energy; and so the energy of the universe tends toward a state of entropy in which matter, having released all its heat, is incapable of further motion. All expenditure of energy, from this point of view, is an irrecoverable loss, a "degradation" of the capacity to do further work. And since "all history must be studied as a science," and "the second law of thermodynamics rules biology with an authority fully as despotic as it asserts in physics," then "the law of thermodynamics must embrace human history," and the historian, in all honesty, must "define his profession as the science of human degradation."

For once, Adams' reasoning, given his premises, is impeccable; the fusion of history and nature is perfect. Of course, the second law of thermodynamics applies only to closed systems, and no one knows whether the universe is closed or has some means of restoring its energy potential. But, despite this qualification, the *Letter* achieves a tenable scientific theory of history. It steers clear of variables that cannot be measured and substances that cannot be defined, and it is empirically verifiable. Its other advantages for Adams' purposes will appear shortly.

Second, the three versions of history assume that the scientific description of reality implies an actual monism. As Adams understood chemistry and physics, their intention was to comprehend the working of the primary substance out of which the universe was made. All other sciences studied the various special forms taken by this substance— the earth, plants, animals, etc.—and since man was but one more form, the science of history was the study of substance too, albeit under peculiar conditions. Being universal and observable, the original substance must be atomic and material; hence when Adams talks of "force" or "energy" in connection with history, he is merely attempting to carry over the general terminology suitable to an atomistic physical reality into a special field of its application.

This "scientific" monism posits a unity not unlike, and possessing many of the intellectual advantages of, what Adams had called the "pantheism" of St. Thomas Aquinas. It is the resolution on an abstract level of concrete multiplicity, and it converts multiplicity from an absolute fact into nothing more than appearance. The drive of Adams' mind toward continuity, toward meaning, thus succeeds in overcoming the chaos that almost swamped the *Education*. By abstracting from the chaos a new unity, Adams made it possible for himself to understand chaos in the only terms that could satisfy him, the terms of rational causality, purposeful movement, and final goal.

Third, monistic unity permits the framing of single, all-inclusive laws. If the ultimate substance is one, then whatever laws it obeys in the laboratory must be valid in all places and times. Adams leaped to the conclusion, too, that the unity of substance meant that only one law was necessary to describe its basic principle of motion. The atom must be innately capable of behaving in only one way; the apparent variety of its modes of behavior in nature must be reducible to one ultimate mode, because reality is one.

The insistence upon unity of law in nature was the very heart of the matter for Adams. Without it he could see little hope for establishing history as a science on an equal footing with physics or chemistry. But it was a source of confusion too, for matter can by no means be stuffed into any one conceptual pigeonhole. Adams was aware of this state of uncertainty in the physical sciences, but he felt, and in this he had the support of some authorities, that the uncertainty was temporary, and that science would soon fix on one of its available hypotheses as the true one. In the meantime, he must plunge ahead and make his choice among the candidates for a universal law of history, hoping that physics would eventually vindicate him.

The result is that each of his three late writings on history is founded on a different law of the behavior of matter. Always watching the "horizon of science," Adams jumped from one law to another as each promised increased certainty. In the *Education* he seems to be primarily relying on a gravitational theory according to which masses of "force" "attract" other masses and change is caused by new forces which upset existing balances and create the need for a new balance among the totality of forces. "The image needed here is that of a new centre, or preponderating mass, artificially introduced on earth in the midst of a system of attractive forces that previously made their own equilibrium, and constantly induced to accelerate its motion till it shall establish a new equilibrium." His theory assumes, Adams goes on to say, that "all history, terrestrial or cosmic, mechanical or intellectual, would be reducible to this formula if we knew the facts." But in the *Rule* a new formula, perhaps not of such readily conceivable universality but more precise in its "image" of change, takes over for history: "Under the Rule of Phase . . . man's Thought, considered as a single substance passing through a series of historical phases, is assumed to follow the analogy of water, and to pass from one phase to another through a series of critical points which are determined by the three factors Attraction, Acceleration, and Volume, for each change of equilibrium."

The *Letter*, starting as always from "the principle that all history must be studied as a science," shifts to a new formula: the law of the degradation of energy. Since all work in nature must be accomplished by the loss of energy, and since history is the accumulated data of the work performed by human individuals and societies, history must necessarily be, in its final meaning, a record of lost and irrecoverable human energy. "From the physicist's point of view, Man, as a conscious and constant, single, natural force, seems to have no function except that of dissipating or degrading energy." From this iron rule there is no escape except by the exemption of man from natural law, which is impermissible. Whatever change in history, then, which would appear to indicate an intensification of human energy rather than its

loss is illusory, the effect of a concentration of dwindling energies
rather than any new gain of energy. The historian, seeking a general
theory of change on the basis of thermodynamic law, must therefore
"treat primitive humanity as a volume of human molecules of un-
equal intensities, tending to dissipate energy, and to correct the loss
by concentrating mankind into a single, dense mass like the sun. History would then become a record of successive phases of contraction,
divided by periods of explosion, tending always towards an ultimate
equilibrium in the form of a volume of human molecules of equal intensity, without coordination."

It is not hard to recognize the familiar mental process which at last
finds a resting place, however uneasy, in a scientific law of history.
Such a law provides Adams with a means of determining the direction
and goal of what is impersonally real. By establishing the continuity of
the past, it projects a continuous line into the future toward a predictable end. The life of mankind can finally be said to have a destination, even if that destination only consists in "an ultimate equilibrium
in the form of a volume of human molecules of equal intensity, without coordination." Adams' most deeply rooted motive, the need to
understand the meaning of life in terms of its end, thus is fulfilled in
scientific law. It is of no significance that he never settled on one law
or one definite end; all are used in the same way and satisfy the same
intellectual requirement. The motive, in fine, dominates the idea, even
to the extent of making nugatory the contradictions and disparities
among its different versions.

Fourth, the historical theory in all of its forms is deterministic. The
assumption of a monism changing according to a single law is equated
in Adams' mind with an irreversible process—history cannot undo itself or retrace its steps. The *Education* says flatly and with some relish
that the "law of acceleration" which determines the speed of human
thought-change under the attractive force of nature is "definite and
constant as any law of mechanics, [and] cannot be supposed to relax
its energy to suit the convenience of man. No one is likely to suggest
a theory that man's convenience had been consulted by Nature at any
time, or that Nature consulted the convenience of any of her crea-
tions." Nature's way is rather that of absolute and irresistible legality;
like St. Thomas' God, it is pre-eminently just and not merciful.

The *Rule* places man in another rigid framework of law. Here
"everything, animate or inanimate, spiritual or material, exists in
Phase; . . . all is equilibrium more or less unstable." History at every
moment is inevitably moving toward its next phase and, "the processes
of History being irreversible," its essential structure is that of a succession of phases following each other as regularly as the links of a chain.
The *Letter* is even more insistent on this theme. Over and over, but-
tressed with a multitude of authoritative references, it repeats its

fundamental axiom, namely "the law of physics that nature, always and everywhere, tends to an equilibruim by levelling its intensities." With every gesture, energy runs out at nature's pores, a finite stock sinking relentlessly to dead level. In the second law of thermodynamics mankind faces its unavoidable destiny. "For human purposes, whatever does work is a form of energy, and since historians exist only to recount and sum up the work that society has done, either as State, or as Church, as civil or as military, as intellectual or physical, organisms, they will, if they obey the physical law, hold that society does work by degrading its energies." Even if it should appear that society has somehow managed to increase its store of energy, to make progress such as evolutionists and historians love to celebrate, this is a deception stemming from the fact that "degradation of energy may create, or convey, an impression of progress and gain." This impression of gain, the true scientific historian knows, "is derived from an impression of Order due to the levelling of energies; but. . . the impression of Order is an illusion consequent on the dissolution of the higher Order which had supplied, by lowering its inequalities, all the useful energies that caused progress. The reality behind the illusion is, therefore, absence of the power to do useful work,—or what man knows in his finite sensibilities as death."

Fifth, each of the last writings contains prophecies, both overt and implied, that are occasioned by Adams' determinism. Many of the foregoing quotations have made it plain that an air of catastrophe hangs over all three. Each concludes in the expectation of doom or of a radical change in the nature or conditions of human life that would be equivalent to doom. The laws that govern historical change admit of no other conclusion. The *Education,* basing its prognosis on the ever accelerating attraction of an infinitely complex nature upon human thought, finds little reason to hope that thought will be adequate to the demands made upon it:

> If any analogy whatever existed between the human mind, on one side, and the laws of motion, on the other, the mind had already entered a field of attraction so violent that it must immediately pass beyond, into new equilibrium, like the Comet of Newton, to suffer dissipation altogether, like meteoroids in the earth's atmosphere. If it behaved like an explosive, it must rapidly recover equilibrium; if it behaved like a vegetable, it must reach its limits of growth; and even if it acted like the earlier creations of energy—the saurians and sharks—it must have nearly reached the limits of its expansion.

Adams was willing to admit uncertainty about just how it *would* behave, but there was no doubt the outcome was going to be unpleasant for mankind.

In the *Rule* Adams foresees two possibilities for thought as it approaches—perhaps in 1917—its next phase, the Ethereal. One is a "subsidence of the current into an ocean of potential thought, or mere consciousness . . . like static electricity." The consequence of this "might be an indefinitely long stationary period" in which "the current would merely cease to flow." Alternatively,

> if, in the prodigiously rapid vibration of its last phases, Thought should continue to act as the universal solvent which it is, and should reduce the forces of the molecule, the atom, and the electron to that costless servitude to which it has reduced the old elements of earth and air, fire and water; if man should continue to set free the infinite forces of nature, and attain the control of cosmic forces on a cosmic scale, the consequences may be as surprising as the change of water to vapor, of the worm to the butterfly, or radium to electrons. At a given volume and velocity, the forces that are concentrated on his head must act.

The vagueness of this action by the forces concentrated on man's head may mitigate its horror to some extent, but the gloomy atmosphere of the *Letter* is wholly unrelieved. Dissolution and death revel on every page. The very creation of man was the act of a decaying nature; every step of his development has been a sign of waning power; every increase in his specialization has brought him closer to helplessness and extinction. "Already the anthropologists have admitted man to be specialized beyond the hope of further variation, so that, as an energy, he must be treated as a weakened Will,—an enfeebled vitality,—a degraded potential." Man's proudest possession, his reason, cannot even be regarded as a source of energy or of hope for the future. Reason is only "a mechanism," an economy of the force of instinct or will that lies behind it, and man's reliance on this makeshift testifies to his growing impotence.

> Very unwillingly can he [the scientific teacher of history] admit Reason to be an energy at all; at the utmost, he can hardly allow it to be more than a passive instrument of a physico-chemical energy called Will;—an ingenious economy in the application of power . . . but if persuaded to concede the intrinsic force of Reason, he must still reject its independence. As a force it must obey the laws of force; as an energy it must content itself with such freedom as the laws of energy allow, and in any case it must submit to the final and fundamental necessity of Degradation.

All must submit to this final and fundamental necessity; there is no escape. The sun itself, having performed this trick in the past, "is ready to condense again at any moment, causing another violent disequilibrium, to be followed by another great outburst and waste of its expiring heat." In such circumstances it is not necessary to try to calculate the date of the impending disaster, as Adams had done in the *Rule*. What must come so certainly may come in its own good time—and perhaps, after all, that will not be a moment too soon. "No one can be trusted to express so much as an opinion about the moment when any special vital process may expect to be reduced in energy; man and beast can, at the best, look forward only to a diversified agony of twenty million years; but at no instant of this considerable period can the professor of mathematics flatter either himself or his students with an exclusive or extended hope of escaping imbecility."

In these strange mutations bred of science and history the mind of Henry Adams reaches a logical terminus. This is not to say that his course and destination were preordained, or that they were in any way necessary, but that they have a rationale, an inner coherence derived from persistent motives and assumptions. These motives and assumptions provided Adams with a range of intellectual possibilities for his mind to explore; and by a series of choices, both conscious and unconscious, he realized certain of these possibilities in his books. Each book exhausts the intellectual content of his choice; each is a step toward exhausting the possibilities of his motives. In his final writings Adams carried his thought to one of the limits inherently possible to it from the start.

In doing so, in reaching the end of his quest, he arrived at a colossal irony. For what Adams discovered was that life had no meaning; the quest ended in a sheer, blank void from which there was no way of escape. Always pressing for certainty, for nothing less than absolute certainty, he found it in universal death, an event no less meaningless than certain. The unity which he had insisted on as a necessary condition of thought turned, in the very moment of its achievement, into an impenetrable chaos; in death, unity and chaos are one. The end which was to give life its form robbed all purpose of significance; the reality which was to give nature its order and history its truth turned nature and history into the merest dream from which humanity would one day wake only to be drowned. The bitter paradox of Adams' career is that the motives which impelled him to brilliant acts of creation were insatiable in their demand for perfection. His last works evidence the craving of a religious mystic for universal dissolution, for an end to the torment of finite intelligence through union with the "ultimate ocean of atoms." More than a decade before, he had predicted the movement of his own mind. "Thought," said the Rajah,

> Travelling in constant circles, round and round,
> Must ever pass through endless contradictions,
> Returning on itself at last, till lost
> In silence.

10

ᵇ THE LIFE OF
GEORGE CABOT LODGE

THE *Education* ends with the faint sounding of a unique and in-
congruous note. Its last sentence reads as follows: "Perhaps some
day—say 1938, their centenary—they [Clarence King, John Hay,
and Henry Adams] might be allowed to return together for a holiday,
to see the mistakes of their own lives made clear in the light of the
mistakes of their successors; and perhaps then, for the first time since
man began his education among the carnivores, they would find a
world that sensitive and timid natures could regard without a shudder." What makes this remark so unexpected is that it follows on the
heels of a lengthy prediction of disaster. The world of 1938 could not
help but be, by Adams' own hypothesis, less hospitable than ever to
sensitive and timid natures. But even more unexpected is the tone of
the author's reference to himself. The *Education* is not free of un-
intended self-pity, but it scrupulously avoids self-excuse. His failure,
Adams insists, was not the result of any special weakness in himself
or of an unfair disadvantage by which he was handicapped in the race
of life. Rather, it proceeded inevitably from the inner disunity caused
by his heritage, his maladjustment to the real world, and the uncontrollable disorder of that world. At the beginning of the *Education* he
rejects the idea that he was innately different from his contemporaries
to any significant degree—"Whatever was peculiar about him was
education, not character." And he declares himself perfectly content
with the cards dealt him by birth: "Probably no child, born in the
year, held better cards than he. . . . To his life as a whole he was a
consenting, contracting party and partner from the moment he was
born to the moment he died."

Yet the last sentence of the *Education* certainly appears to hint
some measure of qualification in Adams' acceptance of the terms on
which life was offered him. For a moment we glimpse the mannikin's
private feelings toward all that has gone before; the discredited ego,
carefully suppressed throughout the long impersonal demonstration
of inevitable failure, has the last word after all, and we are abruptly
left with the dissonant impression of a "sensitive and timid nature"

shuddering at the world in which it finds itself. Adams was nowhere else given to such naked self-revelation in his books; there is no place to fit this impression into the intellectual career that has been traced up to this point. Nevertheless, it strikes the keynote of his last book, a book which can be read as a supplemental autobiography or retrospect of his own life through the medium of someone else's. Its theme is the plight of a sensitive and timid nature in a world it could regard only with a shudder.

George Cabot Lodge was the son of Henry Cabot Lodge, with whom Adams had been on intimate terms ever since the days of his professorship at Harvard. Although the relations between the two older men gradually acquired an undercurrent of mutual repulsion, the younger Lodge was drawn to Adams as a teacher and occasional avuncular companion. Lodge was an exuberantly vital person; he was remembered by Edith Wharton as a brilliant talker; and he was consumed with the ambition to be a great poet. It was this ambition that differentiated him from the Brahmin type which otherwise he might have represented perfectly, and that formed the basis of the sympathy between him and Adams. From Adams he sought approval of his manuscripts, and his mind undoubtedly absorbed more than a tincture of the Adamsian influence. Whether or not this was for the best is hard to say; in any case, Lodge's poetry retains no interesting qualities for the contemporary reader. It is encased in a stiff and abstract rhetoric and suffers from a premature disillusionment with the futility of life. Nevertheless, Lodge wrote with desperate seriousness, and his early death in 1909 seemed to Adams a poignant object lesson on the fate of art in America. Adams wrote the memoir of his young friend diffidently and with no apparent pleasure, at the request of the senior Lodge, and it was published in 1911 as the third volume in the collected works of George Cabot Lodge.

The experience recorded in the *Life of George Cabot Lodge* parallels in many ways that of the *Education*. It is this fact which establishes in the reader's mind a consciousness of the unexpressed identity between the author and his subject. Lodge, like Adams, was a thoroughbred Bostonian whose forebears included men of great distinction in American political life. His youth was shaped by the opposing influences of Boston and Nahant, just as Adams' own had been divided between Quincy and Boston. True to type, he went to Harvard, and then, at twenty-two, to Paris where he continued his studies in the Romance languages and felt occasional guilt at not preparing himself for a useful career—like that of a journalist. He even spent a winter in Berlin and complained of the language. Subsequently he was his father's secretary in Washington and, in the end, having directed all his ambition to literature, he suffered the almost inevitable defeat and failure of the American man of letters.

These similarities are, of course, circumstantial, but they lead to the perception of a fundamental identity. The central meaning of Lodge's life, as Adams sees it, is that he was the victim of American society. The *Life of Lodge* is perhaps the first American work of criticism to take as its motivating idea the inescapable alienation of the artist from society, and it represents that alienation as the cause of the unfulfillment and failure of the artist. It is with this image of the alienated artist that Adams identifies himself in the last of his books.

Adams represents Lodge as having been born into a society in which the very springs of poetry had gone dry: "A poet, born in Boston, in 1873, saw about him a society which commonly bred refined tastes, and often did refined work, but seldom betrayed strong emotions. . . . The twenty-five years between 1873 and 1898—years of astonishing scientific and mechanical activity—were marked by a steady decline of literary and artistic intensity, and especially of the feeling for poetry, which, at best, had never been the favorite form of Boston expression." To the poet of this time and place society could only appear as "the absence of all that he might have supposed it to be, as he read of it in the history and poetry of the past." His own motive was a "suppressed instinct" so far as the people around him were concerned, and therefore, in seeking to liberate the instinct of poetry, his expression naturally took the form of "a reaction against society." Lodge and Boston were not alone in this predicament, for Adams saw it as the universal condition of the art in his time. "Less and less [poetry] appeared, as in earlier ages, the natural, favorite expression of society itself. In the last half of the nineteenth century, the poet became everywhere a rebel against his surroundings. What had been begun by Wordsworth, Byron, and Shelley, was carried on by Algernon Swinburne in London or Paul Verlaine in Paris or Walt Whitman in Washington, by a common instinct of revolt."

The posture of isolated revolt, however, placed an enormous strain on the will of the poet, a strain to which the careers of Swinburne, Verlaine, and Whitman amply testify. For Lodge in Boston, where "the gap between the poet and the citizen was so wide as to be impassable," the strain proved well-nigh fatal. Adams does not hesitate to attribute Lodge's early death in part to the terrible effort that went into sustaining his poetic vitality, an effort made all the more intense by the hopelessness which attended its failure to elicit a response. With each publication he found himself removed farther "in the direction which led away from the regular paths of modern activity"; each book was an act that "widened the gap between himself and his world." The attempt to bridge the gap with his poetry was, by its very nature, ironically foredoomed to accomplish just the opposite, so that as Lodge persisted his "consciousness of losing ground,—of failure to find a larger horizon of friendship beyond his intimacy;—the growing fear that, beyond this narrow range, no friends existed in the immense void of society,—or could exist, in the form of society which he lived in,—the suffocating sense of talking and singing in a vacuum that allowed no echo to return, grew more and more oppressive with each effort to overcome it." Finally, the writing of *Herakles,* his most ambitious piece of work, so exhausted him that, as Adams tells it, he knew himself that "something hung over him which would have some tragic end." Only "the encouragement of great literary success," Adams thinks, "might have helped and stimulated the action of the heart," but such encouragement was not forthcoming and Lodge, at thirty-six, was dead within a year.

The *Life of Lodge* is, on Adams' part, an act of complaint and of self-mourning. Its tone, to be sure, is reserved and cold, rather more so than in any other of his books, as though the author were trying to suppress a sympathy which he feared must inevitably appear sentimental. But it is quite obvious that Lodge's life need not have been treated in the manner Adams chose. The poet's victimization by society, true as it may have been, exists more in the eye of the beholder than in the material beheld. Adams imposes his own definition on Lodge, which is why that definition seems inescapably a projection of himself into his subject. Lodge is made to fit, perhaps unfortunately for him, into a critique of modern life that is fully evolved and can absorb only new matter for illustration. But one further reason for Adams' tendentious treatment of Lodge can appropriately be mentioned in a study of Adams' career as a writer. This was his own failure, as he considered it, to arouse a response in "the immense void of society," to gain the attention of the world beyond the narrow limits of his intimacy.

The letters of Adams' old age give frequent glimpses of his disappointment at the reception accorded his books by critics and public. "My favorite figure of the American author," he wrote Barrett Wendell in 1909, "is that of a man who breeds a favorite dog, which he throws into the Mississippi River for the pleasure of making a splash. The river does not splash, but it drowns the dog." The *History* was a pure-bred animal if there ever was one, but Adams felt keenly that, in terms of reward and influence, he had made far less of a splash than historians whom he did not regard as his intellectual superiors, men like Bancroft, Prescott, Motley and Parkman. He was convinced that he had barely been read, remarking to his brother Brooks in 1905 that "I never yet heard of ten men who had ever read my history," and telling a visitor in 1911 that "nobody had ever read his *History* . . . and that libraries refused to buy it." When the visitor protested that he had heard it praised by "competent authorities," Adams "said that they probably hadn't read it."

After the *History* Adams brought out most of his work privately, and his usual justification was the indifference of the American public. In 1911 he told Mabel Hooper La Farge, "I stopped publishing books twenty years ago because I could not induce anybody to show the least interest in them. No one would even tell me they were bad." And as each book appeared, it was accompanied by disparagements of the audience which was being denied an opportunity to ignore it. Adams simply decided—and here he is very much in the vein of the *Letter to American Teachers of History*—that

> the world outside—the so-called modern world—can only pervert and degrade the conceptions of the primitive instinct of art and feeling, and that our only chance is to accept the limited number of survivors— the one-in-a-thousand of born artists and poets—and to intensify the energy of feeling within that radiant centre. In other words, I am a creature of our poor old Calvinistic, St. Augustinian fathers, and am not afraid to carry out my logic to the rigorous end of regarding our present society, its ideals and purposes, as dregs and fragments of some primitive, essential instinct now nearly lost.

Thus, in his last book, Henry Adams presents himself once again as a failure, this time in a light both more pathetic and more rebellious than before. He was a sensitive and timid nature, born for art in a time when art was a dying instinct, and living the life of a thwarted alien among his uncomprehending fellows. Indeed, the *Life of Lodge* terminates the theme of failure in Adams' works. Lodge's quest was that of the artist seeking in achieved poetic expression the reason for his being. In his failure Adams witnesses and objectifies the ultimate hopelessness of his own life. For after all, and despite his unwillingness to admit it to himself, Adams' career had been that of an artist. All the best of himself—his Puritan integrity, his love of clear, rational form, his power to conceive of life as a disciplined effort to realize impersonal goals—all these, which he had never stopped thinking of as somehow intended for a life of power, had gone into his books as the stuff of art. The *Life of Lodge,* however, is Adams' dismissal of his work as inadequate to redeem the disappointments it had cost him, and it is his curse upon the world that had blighted even this last possibility of success.

SELECTED BIBLIOGRAPHY

NOTE: Works available in paperbound editions are indicated.

ADAMS' CHIEF WORKS

Chapters of Erie and Other Essays. (In collaboration with Charles F. Adams, Jr.) Boston: J. R. Osgood, 1871. (P, selection)

The Life of Albert Gallatin. Philadelphia: Lippincott, 1879.

Democracy An American Novel. (Anon.) New York: Holt, 1880. (P)

John Randolph. Boston and New York: Houghton Mifflin, 1882. (P)

Esther A Novel. Pseudonym, Frances Snow Compton. New York: Holt, 1884. (P)

History of the United States of America during the Administrations of Thomas Jefferson and James Madison. 9 vols. New York: Scribner, 1889–1891. Republished, New York: Antiquarian Press, distributed by Barnes & Noble, 1962. (P, selection)

Historical Essays. New York: Scribner, 1891.

Memoirs of Marau Taaroa, Last Queen of Tahiti, tr. and ed. Henry Adams. No place named: Privately printed, 1893. Republished, revised and enlarged, as *Memoirs of Arii Taimai E,* Paris: Privately printed, 1901.

Mont-Saint-Michel and Chartres. Washington: Privately printed, 1904. (P)

The Education of Henry Adams. Washington: Privately printed, 1907. (P)

The Life of George Cabot Lodge. Boston and New York: Houghton Mifflin, 1911.

The Degradation of the Democratic Dogma, ed. Brooks Adams. New York: Macmillan, 1919. Contains "Tendency of History," *The Rule of Phase Applied to History,* and *A Letter to American Teachers of History.* (P)

ADDITIONAL WORKS

Essays in Anglo-Saxon Law, ed. Henry Adams. Boston: Little, Brown, 1876. Contains Adams' essay "Anglo-Saxon Courts of Law."

Documents Relating to New England Federalism, 1800–1815, ed. Henry Adams. Boston: Little, Brown, 1877.

The Writings of Albert Gallatin, ed. Henry Adams. 3 vols. Philadelphia: Lippincott, 1879. Republished, New York: Antiquarian Press, distributed by Barnes & Noble, 1960.

"Prayer to the Virgin of Chartres," in *Letters to a Niece,* ed. Mabel La Farge. Boston and New York: Houghton Mifflin, 1920.

The Great Secession Winter and Other Essays, ed. George Hochfield. New York: Sagamore, 1958. Contains fourteen essays. (P)

LETTERS

A Cycle of Adams Letters 1861–1865, ed. Worthington C. Ford. 2 vols. Boston and New York: Houghton Mifflin, 1920.

Letters to a Niece and Prayer to the Virgin of Chartres, with a Niece's Memories, ed. Mabel La Farge. Boston and New York: Houghton Mifflin, 1920.

Letters of Henry Adams 1858–1918, ed. Worthington C. Ford. 2 vols. Boston and New York: Houghton Mifflin, 1930–1938.

Henry Adams and His Friends, ed. Harold Dean Cater. Boston: Houghton
Mifflin, 1947.
[A list of works containing letters by Henry Adams is included in the Bibliog-
raphy of Robert A. Hume, *Runaway Star.*]

BIBLIOGRAPHY

Blanck, Jacob. *Bibliography of American Literature,* Vol. I. New Haven:
Yale University Press, 1955.
Leary, Lewis. *Articles on American Literature, 1900–1950.* Durham: Duke
University Press, 1954.
Spiller, Robert E., *et al. Literary History of the United States,* Vol. III, *Bib-
liography.* New York: Macmillan, 1948. *Supplement,* ed. Richard M.
Ludwig. New York: Macmillan, 1959.
[A complete list of Adams' writings to 1891 is contained in the Appendixes of
Ernest Samuels, *The Young Henry Adams* and *Henry Adams: The Mid-
dle Years.*]
[A list of critical writings on Adams to 1950 is contained in Robert A. Hume,
Runaway Star.]

BIOGRAPHY

Adams, James Truslow. *Henry Adams.* New York: Albert and Chas. Boni,
1933.
Samuels, Ernest. *The Young Henry Adams.* Cambridge: Harvard University
Press, 1948.
————. *Henry Adams: The Middle Years.* Cambridge: Harvard University
Press, 1958.
Stevenson, Elizabeth. *Henry Adams, a Biography.* New York: Macmillan,
1956. (P)

CRITICAL AND INTERPRETIVE STUDIES

Full-Length

Baym, Max I. *The French Education of Henry Adams.* New York: Columbia
University Press, 1951.
Hume, Robert A. *Runaway Star: An Appreciation of Henry Adams.* Ithaca:
Cornell University Press, 1951.
Jordy, William H. *Henry Adams: Scientific Historian.* New Haven: Yale Uni-
versity Press, 1952.
Levenson, J. C. *The Mind and Art of Henry Adams.* Boston: Houghton Miff-
lin, 1957.
Wasser, Henry. *The Scientific Thought of Henry Adams.* Thessaloniki: Pri-
vately printed, 1956.

Works Containing Chapters or Sections on Adams

Beach, Joseph Warren. *The Outlook for American Prose.* Chicago: University
of Chicago Press, 1926.
Becker, Carl L. *Every Man His Own Historian.* New York: Crofts, 1935.
Bradford, Gamaliel. *American Portraits, 1875–1900.* Boston and New York:
Houghton Mifflin, 1922.

Brooks, Van Wyck. *New England: Indian Summer, 1865–1915.* New York: Dutton, 1940.

Commager, Henry Steele. *The American Mind.* New Haven: Yale University Press, 1950. (P)

Gabriel, Ralph H. *The Course of American Democratic Thought.* New York: Ronald Press, 1940.

Howe, Irving. *Politics and the Novel.* New York: Horizon, 1957. (P)

Kraus, Michael. *A History of American History.* New York: Farrar & Rinehart, 1937.

More, Paul Elmer. *A New England Group and Others: Shelburne Essays, Eleventh Series.* Boston and New York: Houghton Mifflin, 1921.

Nuhn, Ferner. *The Wind Blew From the East.* New York: Harper, 1942.

Parrington, Vernon Louis. *Main Currents in American Thought,* Vol. III. New York: Harcourt, Brace, 1930. (P)

Speare, Morris Edmund. *The Political Novel.* New York: Oxford University Press, 1924.

Winters, Yvor. *In Defense of Reason.* New York: Swallow Press and William Morrow, 1947.

Wish, Harvey. *The American Historian.* New York: Oxford University Press, 1960.

Recent Critical Articles

Blackmur, Richard P. "The Atlantic Unites," *Hudson Review* (Summer, 1952).

———. "The Harmony of True Liberalism: Henry Adams' *Mont-Saint-Michel and Chartres,*" *Sewanee Review* (Winter, 1952).

Bonner, Thomas N. "Henry Adams: A Sketch and an Analysis," *Historian* (November, 1957).

Cairns, John C. "The Successful Quest of Henry Adams," *South Atlantic Quarterly* (Spring, 1958).

Glicksberg, Charles I. "Henry Adams and the Aesthetic Quest," *Prairie Schooner* (Fall, 1951).

Jordy, William. "Henry Adams and Francis Parkman," *American Quarterly* (Spring, 1951).

Kariel, Henry S. "The Limits of Social Science: Henry Adams' Quest for Order," *American Political Science Review* (December, 1956).

MacLean, Kenneth. "Window and Cross in Henry Adams' *Education,*" *University of Toronto Quarterly* (July, 1959).

Maud, Ralph. "Henry Adams: Irony and Impasse," *Essays in Criticism* (October, 1958).

Mumford, Howard M. "Henry Adams and the Tendency of History," *New England Quarterly* (March, 1959).

Saveth, Edward N. "The Heroines of Henry Adams," *American Quarterly* (Fall, 1956).

Wasser, Henry. "The Thought of Henry Adams," *New England Quarterly* (December, 1951).

White, Lynn, Jr. "Dynamo and Virgin Reconsidered," *American Scholar* (Spring, 1958).

INDEX

Characters from Adams' works are entered in small capital letters.